# Table of Contents

Introduction.................................................................................... 7

What is Vegetarianism?...................................................................... 7

The earliest record of vegetarianism...................................................... 7

Comparison of vegetarian and semi-vegetarian diets................................ 8

Health effects of Vegetarianism........................................................... 8

Medical use.................................................................................... 8

Ethics and Vegetarian diet.................................................................. 9

What is Instant Pot?.......................................................................... 9

Is Instant Pot The Best Pressure Cooker?................................................ 9

How long does it take for instant pot to come to pressure?........................... 9

Instant Pot vs Pressure Cooker............................................................. 10

A P P E T I Z E R S............................................................................ 11

   "Baked" Cauliflower with Spicy Tomato Sauce (Instant Pot).................... 11

   Breaded Carrot Fries (Instant Pot).................................................... 12

   Chervil Potato in Tomato Sauce....................................................... 14

   Easy Herbed Risotto (Instant Pot)..................................................... 15

   Indian Flavorful and Tangy Potato Appetizer........................................ 17

   Spicy Broccoli with Parmesan Appetizer (Instant Pot)............................ 18

   Spicy Spinach with Herbed Mustard Leaves (Instant Pot)........................ 20

   Traditional Greek Giant Beans (Instant Pot)......................................... 21

   Truffle Potatoes with Parmesan (Instant Pot)........................................ 23

   Vegetable Saffron Stir-fry (Instant Pot).............................................. 24

B R E A K F A S T.............................................................................. 26

"Spooky" Scrambled Eggs (Instant Pot)..................................................26

Breakfast Vegetable Pie (Instant Pot)..................................................28

Delicious Porridge with Banana (Instant Pot)..................................................29

Green Vegetable Quiche (Instant Pot)..................................................31

Light Vegetable Breakfast Cake (Instant Pot)..................................................33

Mushroom Omelette with Pecorino Romano (Instant Pot)..................................................34

Olives and Sun-dried Tomato Bread (Instant Pot)..................................................36

Popeye Cream Breakfast (Instant Pot)..................................................37

Porridge with Pumpkin Seeds and Berries (Instant Pot)..................................................39

Savory Oat Porridge with Vegetables (Instant Pot)..................................................40

L U N C H..................................................42

Chaomi Rice with Tamari Sauce (Instant Pot..................................................42

Chilly Red Potato Salad with Mayonnaise (Instant Pot)..................................................43

Creamy Sweet Potatoes Mash (Instant Pot)..................................................45

Delicious Creamy Tomato Soup (Instant Pot)..................................................46

Fava and Mushrooms with Wine Stew (Instant Pot)..................................................48

Full Protein Quinoa Pilaf (Instant Pot)..................................................49

Italian Vegetable Soup with Rice (Instant Pot)..................................................51

Mediterranean Creamy Carrot Soup (Instant Pot)..................................................53

Minestrone Tortellini with Parmesan Cheese (Instant Pot)..................................................55

Mustard Greens Sour "Stew" (Instant Pot)..................................................56

Red Beans and Mushroom Stew (Instant Pot)..................................................58

Spicy Brussels sprouts with Siracha Sauce..................................................60

Spinach Puree with Almonds (Instant Pot)..................................................61

Tasty Corn Soup (Instant Pot)..................................................63

Zucchini Noodles with Goat Cheese (Instant Pot)..................................................65

D I N N E R.................................................................................67

   "Baked" Okra with Grated Tomatoes (Instant Pot).......................................67

   "Grilled" Zucchini with Garlic and Herbs (Instant Pot)..............................69

   Broad beans, Lentils and Peas Cream (Instant Pot)..................................70

   Brown Rice and Lentils with Cheddar Soup (Instant Pot)............................72

   Chickpeas with Tomato, Mushrooms and Avocado Stew (Instant Pot)...........74

   Curried Carrots with Fresh Cream (Instant Pot).....................................76

   Gourmet Fettuccine Alfredo (Instant Pot)..............................................77

   Levantine Vegetarian Dish with Rice (Instant Pot)..................................79

   Mushroom Fettuccini with Sun-dried Tomato (Instant Pot).......................80

   Penne with Collard Greens (Instant Pot).............................................82

   Perfect Cauliflower Rice with Herbs (Instant Pot)..................................84

   Red and Green Beans Stew (Instant Pot).............................................85

   Rizi-Bizi with Peas Risotto (Instant Pot).............................................87

   The Simplest Pasta with Broccoli (Instant Pot).....................................89

   Zesty Quinoa with Lime Coconut (Instant Pot).....................................90

S N A C K S...............................................................................92

   "Roasted" Sweet Potato Wedges (Instant Pot).......................................92

   Baby Potatoes with Fresh Herbs (Instant Pot).......................................93

   Catalan Breaded Eggplant (Instant Pot)..............................................95

   Cheesy Kale Chips (Instant Pot).......................................................97

   Crunchy Plantain Chips (Instant Pot)..................................................98

   Cumin Sesame Pasta Cauliflower (Instant Pot)......................................100

   Curried Carrot Chips (Instant Pot).....................................................101

   Easy Beetroot Chips (Instant Pot).....................................................103

   Ginger Butternut Squash Chips (Instant Pot)........................................104

Parsnip Fingers with Rosemary (Instant Pot).................................................106

SIDE DISH.................................................................................108

"Roasted" Jerusalem Artichokes with Parsley (Instant Pot)..................... 108

Apple Mango Coleslaw (Instant Pot)............................................. 109

Classic Vegetable Sauerkraut (Instant Pot)..................................... 111

Creamy Pumpkin Squash Soup (Instant Pot)....................................... 112

Mushrooms and Almond Gravy (Instant Pot)....................................... 114

Pepper Squash Puree (Instant Pot............................................... 115

Sweet and Sour Beet Salad (Instant Pot)........................................ 117

Sweet Potato & Pecans Casserole (Instant Pot)................................. 119

Sweet Potato Puree (Instant Pot)............................................... 121

Zucchini and Potato Puree (Instant Pot)........................................ 122

PASTA.................................................................... 124

"Baked" Fusilli with Spinach and Lemon (Instant Pot).......................... 124

Appetizing Balsamic Pasta Salad (Instant Pot)................................. 125

Cold Pasta with Potatoes and Pesto (Instant Pot)..............................127

Double Cheese and Jalapeno Rigatoni (Instant Pot)............................ 128

Farfalle with Peas, Corn and Tartar Sauce (Instant Pot)....................... 130

Lemon-Mint Pasta with Peas and Artichokes (Instant Pot)....................... 132

Pasta Salad with Vegetables and Yogurt Dressing (Instant Pot)................. 133

Pasta with Black Olives and Pine Nuts......................................... 135

Pasta with Colorful Peppers and Tomato (Instant Pot).......................... 137

Penne with Zucchini and Pesto (Instant Pot)...................................139

SAUCES/DIP............................................................... 141

Aromatic Marinara Sauce (Instant Pot)......................................... 141

Cheesemania Dip (Instant Pot).................................................. 143

Cherry - Raspberry Sauce (Instant Pot)............................................144

Creamy Artichoke and Spinach Dip (Instant Pot)..................146

Fresh Mushroom Sauce (Instant Pot)..................................... 147

Honey Quince and Apple Sauce (Instant Pot)........................149

Mandarin Peach Sauce (Instant Pot).......................................150

Marinated Artichoke Dip (Instant Pot)...................................152

Moroccan Pearl Onion Sauce (Instant Pot)........................... 153

Roasted Red Peppers and Basil-Nuts Dressing (Instant Pot)....155

S W E E T S...............................................................................156

4 Ingredients Cornbread Cake (Instant Pot............................. 156

Choco - Maraschino Cherries Cake (Instant Pot)...................158

Chocolate Bread with Hazelnuts (Instant Pot)....................... 160

Coffee Chocolate Mint Bundt  Cake (Instant Pot).................162

Fast Mayo Chocolate Cake (Instant Pot)................................164

Lucuma and Chia Seeds Pudding (Instant Pot)......................165

Perfect Tea Cake (Instant Pot)................................................167

Sweet Cake Mix  (Instant Pot)...............................................169

Total Matte Chocolate Cake (Instant Pot)..............................170

Traditional Rice Pudding (Instant Pot)...................................172

Conclusion............................................................................173

# Introduction

Chomp, chomp, chomp the stalk; nibble, nibble, nib the leaf. Becoming a vegetarian is a great idea and with Instant Pot it becomes a sublime cooking experience that makes the mouth water and the heart dance with joy. There is a whole universe of delicious and nutritious vegetarian dishes out there and they've just become possible because now we're cooking with Instant Pot!

## What is Vegetarianism?

Vegetarianism is the best way to purge the body of all the accumulated toxins that've been piling up over the course of years and decades. By eating only our humble plant friends, we starve the bacteria, fungi and all sorts of baddies skulking inside the body and strengthen our immune system to finally get rid of them. It takes a little bit of persistence to reboot the body's internal self-cleaning systems but once that happens the benefits become obvious: smaller waist size, lower blood sugar, lower blood pressure and so, so much more. There is no such pill or surgery that cleanses the body the same way a rutabaga or radish can.

## The earliest record of vegetarianism

Plenty of written records hailing from India and ancient Greece 700 years before the Christ era speak at length about vegetarianism and tolerance towards animals. This is how we can track the state of those societies and find out they really were advanced thinkers. The ideas of a vegetarian lifestyle largely disappeared from Europe after that but they are still going strong in India, which has them deeply embedded in daily life. The modern upsurge of vegetarianism can probably be linked to environmental concerns and the desire to leave a habitable planet for the next generation. Whatever the cause might be, being vegetarian is a win-win for everyone involved.

# Comparison of vegetarian and semi-vegetarian diets

There are many different ways to implement a vegetarian diet into one's life, which led to the rise of semi-vegetarian diets. These include ovo vegetarians (may eat eggs), lacto vegetarians (may eat dairy) and ovo-Lacto vegetarians (may eat both eggs and dairy). The main purpose of these semi-vegetarian diets is to make a vegetarian diet approachable to people who otherwise wouldn't even consider it. As with all other diets, the main principle is to make the vegetarian or semi-vegetarian diet as comfortable as it can be to the dieter.

# Health effects of Vegetarianism

The modern processed food we have so much of is laden with chemicals and various byproducts. These don't pose an immediate danger to our health, which makes them even more dangerous in the long run over decades of such diet. For example, MSG (monosodium glutamate) is a taste enhancer added to canned food and soups to mask the tinny aftertaste that can also cause muscle tightness, headaches, and weakness. The food manufacturers don't necessarily mean to harm the customers – they merely want to cut as many corners as possible while making as many profits. By switching over to vegetarianism we give our body a much-needed respite while fortifying it with powerful plant-based nutrients.

# Medical use

Vegetarianism can be used for medical purposes, though this should always go hand in hand with conventional medicine for the fastest recovery possible. The best possible outcome of any vegetarian diet is a loss of excess body fat through extremely filling plant-based meals that are low in calories and high in dietary fiber. Simply ramping up the dietary fiber intake itself justifies switching over to a vegetarian diet and is enough to deal with a whole host of health issues related to digestion, since dietary fiber swells inside the intestines, stimulates bowel movement and helps eliminate toxins. Again, industrial food makers eliminate dietary fiber from their products because it makes them slower to cook and tougher to chew – they simply can't afford to sell healthy food.

## Ethics and Vegetarian diet

Being a vegetarian can come with a side dish of righteousness, which in this case involves not wanting to harm any animal or even any plant. The latter are called fruitarians, eat exclusively fruit and believe that anything other than picking a fruit is actually doing harm to the plants or microbes living on the plant surface. There are several other varieties of the same belief and all of them are valid as long as they're not imposed on anyone and don't cause undue stress on the dieter. Also note that some extremely restrictive versions of vegetarianism may need vitamin and protein supplements to avoid serious health problems further down the line.

## What is Instant Pot?

Instant Pot is a vegetarian's best friend in the kitchen. This multi-use programmable pressure cooker replaces pressure cooker, sauté pan, slow cooker, rice cooker, steamer, yogurt maker and food warmer. It's tough, robust and yet with a delicate LED display at the front that shows time remaining and allows the user to switch from cooking beans to making a cake in just a couple presses.

## Is Instant Pot The Best Pressure Cooker?

Instant Pot is the best pressure cooker for newbies to learn the ropes and for experts to whip up a delicious meal in no time. Whatever your experience level with pressure cookers, you'll find it a reliable and easy to use multi-functional kitchen helper.

How long does it take for instant pot to come to pressure?
This depends on whether we're using hot or cold liquid and food ingredients. For example, a frozen piece of meat may delay the pressure buildup up to 20 minutes while using hot stock may bring it down to merely 2. Whenever possible, use food ingredients that are room temperature.

## Instant Pot vs Pressure Cooker

Instant Pot is a proprietary pressure cooker brand that's a fruit of genuine love that brought engineering and cuisine to a wonderful union that delights and exhilarates the entire world. Be fearless, explore the whole universe of aromas and flavors Instant Pot can produce and discover in yourself the culinary abilities you didn't even know you had. Savor every moment spent with your Instant Pot and every ounce of delicious vegetarian meals it made for you and your loved ones.

In the next chapter, we will present you 100 healthy, hearty vegetarian Instant Pot recipes. We hope you'll enjoy it. **Bon appétit!**

# APPETIZERS

## "Baked" Cauliflower with Spicy Tomato Sauce (Instant Pot)

## Ingredients

- 2 Tbsp garlic infused olive oil
- 1 1/2 lbs of cauliflower
- 1 cup tomato sauce
- 1 tsp turmeric
- 1 tsp cumin
- 1 tsp cayenne pepper
- Salt to taste
- 1 cup water

## Instructions

1. Wash and cut the cauliflower into small pieces.
2. Place all ingredients in Instant Pot's inner pot/liner; stir with wooden spoon.
3. Lock lid into place and set on the MANUAL setting for 4 minutes.
4. When the timer beeps, press "Cancel" and carefully flip the Quick Release valve to let the pressure out.
5. Taste and adjust salt and pepper.
6. Serve.

**Servings:** 6

**Cooking Times**

Total Time: 15 minutes

**Nutrition Facts**

Serving size: 1/6 of a recipe (7 ounces).

Percent daily values based on the Reference Daily Intake (RDI) for a 2000 calorie diet.

Nutrition information calculated from recipe ingredients.

**Amount Per Serving**

Calories 81,49

Calories From Fat (55%) 44,47

**% Daily Value**

Total Fat 5,06g 8%

Saturated Fat 0,73g 4%

Cholesterol 0mg 0%

Sodium 346,97mg 14%

Potassium 496,24mg 14%

Total Carbohydrates 8,4g 3%

Fiber 3,08g 12%

Sugar 3,95g

Protein 2,84g 6%

# Breaded Carrot Fries (Instant Pot)

## Ingredients

- 1 lb Carrots sliced into 1/4-inch rounds
- 1/2 cup all-purpose flour
- 1/4 cup breadcrumbs, plane
- 2 Tbs butter
- 1 large egg

## Instructions

1. Combine the flour, breadcrumbs, salt, and pepper. Set aside.
2. In a separate bowl, beat egg; set aside
3. Press SAUTÉ button on your Instant Pot and heat the butter.
4. Dip each carrot in the egg mixture and then roll it in the flour mixture.
5. Once butter is melted, place prepared carrots in your Instant Pot.
6. Lock lid into place and set on the MANUAL setting for 3 minutes.
7. When the timer beeps, press "Cancel" and carefully flip the Quick Release valve to let the pressure out.
8. Serve hot.

**Servings:** 4

**Cooking Times**

Total Time: 10 minutes

**Nutrition Facts**

Serving size: 1/4 of a recipe (6 ounces).

Percent daily values based on the Reference Daily Intake (RDI) for a 2000 calorie diet.

Nutrition information calculated from recipe ingredients.

**Amount Per Serving**

Calories 192,01

Calories From Fat (35%) 67,02

**% Daily Value**

Total Fat 7,61g 12%

Saturated Fat 4,17g 21%          Total Carbohydrates 26,22g 9%

Cholesterol 61,77mg 21%          Fiber 4,01g 16%

Sodium 156,71mg 7%               Sugar 5,91g

Potassium 317,66mg 9%            Protein 4,87g 10%

# Chervil Potato in Tomato Sauce

## Ingredients

- 4 Tbs Olive oil
- 1 onion finely chopped
- 2 clove garlic, finely chopped
- 4 large potatoes
- 1 cup tomato paste (fresh or canned)

- 1 Tbs dry Chervil
- 1 cup water
- 1/2 tsp fresh parsley, chopped
- 1/2 tsp Salt and pepper to taste

## Instructions

1. Press SAUTÉ button on your Instant Pot and heat the oil.
2. Sauté the onion and garlic with a pinch of salt for 3 - 4 minutes.
3. Add potatoes and tomatoes and sauté for 2 - 3 minutes.
4. Add all remaining ingredients and season salt and pepper.
5. Lock lid into place and set on the MANUAL setting for 10 minutes.
6. After the pressure cooking time has finished using Natural Release - it takes 10 - 25 minutes to depressurize naturally.
7. Taste and adjust seasonings to taste.
8. Serve warm.

**Servings**: 6

**Cooking Times**

Total Time: 40 minutes

**Nutrition Facts**

Serving size: 1/6 of a recipe (8 ounces)

Percent daily values based on the Reference Daily Intake (RDI) for a 2000 calorie diet.

Nutrition information calculated from recipe ingredients.

**Amount Per Serving**

Calories 209,51

Calories From Fat (39%) 82,01

**% Daily Value**

Total Fat 9,29g 14%

Saturated Fat 1,32g 7%

Cholesterol 0mg 0%

Sodium 233,78mg 10%

Potassium 876,25mg 25%

Total Carbohydrates 29,61g 10%

Fiber 4,36g 17%

Sugar 5,55g

Protein 4,16g 8%

# Easy Herbed Risotto (Instant Pot)

## Ingredients

- 1/4 cup butter
- 1 cup onion
- 2 green onions

- 1 tsp minced garlic (can use more or less)
- 2 cups long-grain rice, (parboiled)

- 3 Tbs vegetable broth
- 1 tsp sweet pepper powder
- 2 tsp hot pepper powder
- 2 Tbs fresh mint, chopped

- Leek, laurel, fresh or dry, mix
- 1 Tbs olive oil
- Salt and ground black pepper to taste

## Instructions

1. Press SAUTÉ button on your Instant Pot and heat the butter.
2. Sauté the onion, green onion and garlic with a pinch of salt and pepper; stir.
3. Add the rice and all remaining ingredients and stir well.
4. Lock lid into place and set on and select the "RICE" button for 10 minutes.
5. When ready, use Natural Release - it takes 10 - 25 minutes to depressurize naturally.
6. Taste and adjust seasonings to taste.
7. Serve warm or cold.

**Servings:** 6

**Cooking Times**

Total Time: 40 minutes

**Nutrition Facts**

Serving size: 1/6 of a recipe (4.5 ounces)

Percent daily values based on the Reference Daily Intake (RDI) for a 2000 calorie diet.

Nutrition information calculated from recipe ingredients.

**Amount Per Serving**

Calories 175,13

Calories From Fat (51%) 90,06

**% Daily Value**

Total Fat 10,24g 16%

Saturated Fat 5,25g 26%

Cholesterol 20,41mg 7%

Sodium 54,63mg 2%

Potassium 94,28mg 3%

Total Carbohydrates 18,86g 6%

Fiber 0,98g 4%

Protein 2,14g 4%

Sugar 1,35g

# Indian Flavorful and Tangy Potato Appetizer

## Ingredients

- 1/4 cup olive oil
- 1 Tbs cumin seeds
- 1 Tbs coriander seeds, pounded
- 5 cloves
- 1 bay leaf
- 1 tsp salt

- 1 tsp red chili powder
- 1 tsp turmeric powder
- 1 tsp dry pomegranate powder
- 2 tsp dried fenugreek leaves
- 5 Potatoes - boiled and cubed

## Instructions

1. Press SAUTÉ button on your Instant Pot and heat 2 tablespoon oil.
2. Place all spices on the list and sauté for 2 minutes: stir well.
3. Add the potatoes and coat them well with the spices.
4. Cancel the Sauté mode.
5. Lock lid into place and set on the MANUAL setting for 3 minutes.
6. Use Quick Release - turn the valve from sealing to venting to release the pressure.
7. Serve warm or cold.

**Servings:** 6

**Cooking Times**

Total Time: 10 minutes

**Nutrition Facts**

Serving size: 1/6 of a recipe (7 ounces)

Percent daily values based on the Reference Daily Intake (RDI) for a 2000 calorie diet.

Nutrition information calculated from recipe ingredients.

**Amount Per Serving**

Calories 234,33

Calories From Fat (39%) 90,32

**% Daily Value**

Total Fat 10,28g 16%

Saturated Fat 1,48g 7%

Cholesterol 0mg 0%

Sodium 406,46mg 17%

Potassium 769,02mg 22%

Total Carbohydrates 33,78g 11%

Fiber 5,95g 24%

Sugar 3,22g

Protein 4,63g 9%

# Spicy Broccoli with Parmesan Appetizer (Instant Pot)

## Ingredients

- 1 cup extra-virgin olive oil

- 4 cloves garlic, smashed

- 1 1/2 lb broccoli stemmed and cut into florets

- 1 tsp crushed red chili flakes
- 1 cup water
- Kosher salt, to taste
- 3/4 cup Parmesan shredded

## Instructions

1. Press SAUTÉ button on your Instant Pot and heat the oil.
2. Sauté the garlic with a pinch of salt for 3 - 4 minutes; stir.
3. Add the cauliflower, salt and pepper, pepper flakes and water; stir well.
4. Lock lid into place and set on the MANUAL setting for 4 minutes.
5. When the timer beeps, press "Cancel" and carefully flip the Quick Release valve to let the pressure out.
6. Sprinkle with Parmesan cheese and serve.

**Servings**: 6

**Cooking Times**

Total Time: 15 minutes

**Nutrition Facts**

Serving size: 1/6 of a recipe (7 ounces)

Percent daily values based on the Reference Daily Intake (RDI) for a 2000 calorie diet.

Nutrition information calculated from recipe ingredients.

**Amount Per Serving**

Calories 172,92

Calories From Fat (66%) 114,74

**% Daily Value**

Total Fat 13,04g 20%

Saturated Fat 3,48g 17%

Cholesterol 11mg 4%

Sodium 273,92mg 11%

Potassium 442,46mg 13%

Total Carbohydrates 8,05g 3%

Fiber 0,1g <1%

Sugar 0,33g

Protein 8,73g 17%

# Spicy Spinach with Herbed Mustard Leaves (Instant Pot)

## Ingredients

- 2 Tbs butter or ghee
- 2 onions, diced
- 1/4 cup minced garlic
- 1 tsp salt and black pepper (or to taste)
- 1 tsp garam masala
- 1 tsp turmeric

- 1 tsp coriander
- 1 tsp ground cumin
- 1 lb spinach, rinsed
- 1 lb mustard leaves, rinsed
- pinch of dried fenugreek leaves

## Instructions

1. Press SAUTÉ button on your Instant Pot and melt the butter or ghee.
2. Add the onion, garlic, and spices; saute for 2-3 minutes.
3. Add the spinach and the mustard greens and stir well.
4. Lock lid into place and set on the MANUAL setting for 15 minutes.
5. Use Natural Release - it takes 10 - 25 minutes to depressurize naturally.
6. Remove the lid and use an immersion blender to puree the contents of the pot.
7. Add a pinch of dried fenugreek leaves.
8. Serve.

**Servings:** 6

**Cooking Times**

Total Time: 50 minutes

## Nutrition Facts

Serving size: 1/6 of a recipe (7 ounces)

Percent daily values based on the Reference Daily Intake (RDI) for a 2000 calorie diet.

Nutrition information calculated from recipe ingredients.

**Amount Per Serving**

Calories 134,07

Calories From Fat (48%) 64,6

**% Daily Value**

| | |
|---|---|
| Total Fat 7,65g 12% | Total Carbohydrates 13,47g 4% |
| Saturated Fat 2,66g 13% | Fiber 4,53g 18% |
| Cholesterol 10,18mg 3% | Sugar 2,08g |
| Sodium 1003,16mg 42% | Protein 6,43g 13% |
| Potassium 569,51mg 16% | |

# Traditional Greek Giant Beans (Instant Pot)

## Ingredients

- 1/2 cup olive oil
- 1 onion sliced
- 2 cloves  garlic crushed or minced
- 1 red sweet pepper
- 1 small hot pepper (optional)
- 2 small carrots, sliced

- 1 lb giants beans
- 1 Tbsp celery (chopped)
- 2 tomatoes, chopped
- 1 Tbs of tomato sauce, low sodium
- 1/2 tsp Salt and ground black pepper
- 3/4 tsp sweet paprika
- 1/2 tsp oregano
- 1 cup vegetable broth

## Instructions

1. Soak the giant beans overnight.
2. Press SAUTÉ button on your Instant Pot and heat the oil.
3. Saute the onion, garlic, sweet pepper, carrots and hot pepper (if used) with a pinch of salt for 3 - 4 minutes.
4. Rinse the giant beans and place in your Instant Pot along with remaining ingredients and stir well.
5. Season salt and pepper and stir again.
6. Lock lid into place and set on the MANUAL setting for 25 minutes.
7. After the pressure cooking time has finished using Natural Release - it takes 10 - 25 minutes to depressurize naturally.
8. Taste and adjust seasonings to taste.
9. Serve warm or cold.

**Servings:** 8

**Cooking Times**

Total Time: 55 minutes

**Nutrition Facts**

Serving size: 1/8 of a recipe (7 ounces)

Percent daily values based on the Reference Daily Intake (RDI) for a 2000 calorie diet.

Nutrition information calculated from recipe ingredients.

**Amount Per Serving**

Calories 355,85

Calories From Fat (36%) 129,42

**% Daily Value**

Total Fat 14,67g 23%

Saturated Fat 2,13g 11%

Cholesterol 0,31mg <1%

Sodium 244,19mg 10%

Potassium 1289,05mg 37%

Total Carbohydrates 43,56g 15%

Fiber 10,74g 43%

Sugar 4,64g

Protein 14,84g 30%

# Truffle Potatoes with Parmesan (Instant Pot)

## Ingredients

- 1/2 cup butter, melted
- 3 lbs potatoes sliced
- 1/4 tsp Salt and pepper to taste

- 1 cup Grated Parmesan cheese
- 1/2 tsp truffle oil
- 1 Tbsp fresh parsley and cilantro, chopped

## Instructions

1. Press SAUTÉ button on your Instant Pot and heat the butter.
2. Place the potatoes and saute with salt and pepper, stirring with wooden spoon, for 2 - 3 minutes
3. Sprinkle with Parmesan cheese and some truffle oil.
4. Lock lid into place and set on the MANUAL setting for 10 minutes.
5. When ready, use Natural Release - it takes 10 - 25 minutes to depressurize naturally.
6. Sprinkle with chopped parsley and cilantro and serve.

**Servings:** 8

**Cooking Times**

Total Time: 55 minutes

**Nutrition Facts**

Serving size: 1/8 of a recipe (7 ounces)

Percent daily values based on the Reference Daily Intake (RDI) for a 2000 calorie diet.

Nutrition information calculated from recipe ingredients.

**Amount Per Serving**

Calories 289,21

Calories From Fat (47%) 136,38

**% Daily Value**

Total Fat 15,52g 24%

Saturated Fat 9,53g 48%

Cholesterol 41,5mg 14%

Sodium 275,89mg 11%

Potassium 738,23mg 21%

Total Carbohydrates 30,26g 10%

Fiber 3,76g 15%

Sugar 1,45g

Protein 8,38g 17%

# Vegetable Saffron Stir-fry (Instant Pot)

## Ingredients

- 1/4 cup extra virgin olive oil
- 1 onion, diced

- 3 cloves garlic, minced
- 1 lb potatoes, peeled and cubed
- 1/2 head of cauliflower, cut into florets
- 1 cup vegetable broth
- 1 cup water
- 1 cup fresh diced tomatoes
- 2 pinch of saffron threads
- 2 medium zucchini, diced
- 1 cup green olives, pitted and chopped
- 3 Tbs fresh parsley, chopped
- 2 tsp cumin
- 2 tsp cinnamon
- Salt and pepper, to taste

## Instructions

1. Pour the oil and place all ingredients to your Instant Pot's inner pot/liner; stir well to combine all ingredients.
2. Lock lid into place and set on the STEAM setting for 10 minutes.
3. When the timer beeps, use Natural Release - it takes 10 - 25 minutes to depressurize naturally.
4. Taste and adjust salt and pepper to taste.
5. Serve warm.

**Servings:** 6

**Cooking Times**

Total Time: 40 minutes

**Nutrition Facts**

Serving size: 1/6 of a recipe (11 ounces).

Percent daily values based on the Reference Daily Intake (RDI) for a 2000 calorie diet.

Nutrition information calculated from recipe ingredients.

**Amount Per Serving**

Calories 166,88

Calories From Fat (66%) 110,36

**% Daily Value**

Total Fat 12,59g 19%

Saturated Fat 1,8g 9%

Cholesterol 0,41mg <1%

Sodium 487,72mg 20%

Potassium 383,51mg 11%

Total Carbohydrates 12,73g 4%

Fiber 3,32g 13%

Sugar 3,46g

Protein 2,81g 6%

# BREAKFAST

## "Spooky" Scrambled Eggs (Instant Pot)

### Ingredients

- 6 eggs
- 1 1/4 cups of milk
- Salt to taste
- 1 Tbs olive oil
- 1 cup water

### Instructions

1. Whisk the eggs, milk, and salt in a bowl.
2. Grease with olive oil a baking dish and pour the egg mixture.
3. Add water to the inner stainless steel pot in the Instant Pot, and place the trivet inside.
4. Place baking dish on the top of the trivet.
5. Lock lid into place and set on the MANUAL setting for 5 minutes.

6. When the timer beeps, press "Cancel" and carefully flip the Quick Release valve to let the pressure out.
7. Transfer eggs on a serving platter and serve immediately.

**Servings**: 4

**Cooking Times**

Total Time: 15 minutes

**Nutrition Facts**

Serving size: 1/4 of a recipe (8 ounces)

Percent daily values based on the Reference Daily Intake (RDI) for a 2000 calorie diet.

Nutrition information calculated from recipe ingredients.

**Amount Per Serving**

Calories 175,21

Calories From Fat (61%) 107,61

**% Daily Value**

Total Fat 12,02g 18%

Saturated Fat 3,77g 19%

Cholesterol 285,1mg 95%

Sodium 289,53mg 12%

Potassium 210,91mg 6%

Total Carbohydrates 4,2g 1%

Fiber 0g 0%

Sugar 4,14g

Protein 11,94g 24%

# Breakfast Vegetable Pie (Instant Pot)

## Ingredients

- 2 carrots sliced
- 2 small potatoes sliced
- 2 small zucchini sliced
- 2 Tbs of extra virgin olive oil
- Salt and pepper to taste

- 1 tsp fresh thyme finely
- 1 pound puff pastry
- 1 cup Cheddar cheese
- 1 cup water

## Instructions

1. Wash, dry and peel the vegetables, cut into small pieces or thin slices.
2. Place the vegetables in a saucepan with the oil, thyme and salt and pepper; sauté for 3 minutes.
3. Remove from heat and set aside.
4. Roll out the puff pastry, place it on the baking dish lined with the parchment paper.
5. Sprinkle the Cheddar cheese and layer a sauté vegetables evenly on a puff pastry.
6. Add water to the inner stainless steel pot in the Instant Pot, and place the trivet inside.
7. Place a baking dish on a trivet.
8. Lock lid into place and set on the MANUAL setting for 5 minutes.
9. When the timer beeps, press "Cancel" and carefully flip the Quick Release valve to let the pressure out.
10. Carefully open the lid and let cool for 10 minutes.
11. Serve.

**Servings**: 8

## Cooking Times

Total Time: 25 minutes

## Nutrition Facts

Serving size: 1/8 of a recipe (6 ounces)

Percent daily values based on the Reference Daily Intake (RDI) for a 2000 calorie diet.

Nutrition information calculated from recipe ingredients.

## Amount Per Serving

Calories 224,35

Calories From Fat (52%) 116,14

## % Daily Value

Total Fat 13,05g 20%

Saturated Fat 5,1g 26%

Cholesterol 14,83mg 5%

Sodium 270,5mg 11%

Potassium 406,55mg 12%

Total Carbohydrates 20,85g 7%

Fiber 2,4g 10%

Sugar 2,81g

Protein 6,76g 14%

# Delicious Porridge with Banana (Instant Pot)

## Ingredients

- 1/4 cup Oatmeal

- 1 1/4 cup milk

- 2 pinch of cinnamon
- 1 banana sliced
- 4 Tbsp sugar

## Instructions

1. Add the oatmeal, milk, cinnamon, and sugar in Instant Pot's inner pot; stir well.
2. Lock lid into place and set on the MANUAL setting for 15 minutes.
3. When the timer beeps, press "Cancel" and carefully flip the Quick Release valve to let the pressure out.
4. Pour a porridge into serving bowls, decorate with banana slices and serve immediately.

**Servings:** 4

**Cooking Times**

Total Time: 20 minutes

**Nutrition Facts**

Serving size: 1/4 of a recipe (5 ounces)

Percent daily values based on the Reference Daily Intake (RDI) for a 2000 calorie diet.

Nutrition information calculated from recipe ingredients.

**Amount Per Serving**

Calories 132,68

Calories From Fat (13%) 17,12

**% Daily Value**

Total Fat 1,94g 3%

Saturated Fat 1,05g 5%

Cholesterol 6,1mg 2%

Sodium 36,58mg 2%

Potassium 231,55mg 7%

Total Carbohydrates 26,54g 9%

Fiber 1,35g 5%

Sugar 20,09g

Protein 3,51g 7%

# Green Vegetable Quiche (Instant Pot)

## Ingredients

- 15 large free range eggs
- 1 1 cups  milk full fat
- 2 cups fresh spinach, chopped
- 1 small onion, finely chopped
- 2 cloves garlic, minced

- 5 white mushrooms finely sliced
- 1 1 tsp of baking powder
- 1 Tbsp Ghee, as required to grease the dish
- 1/2 tsp Sea salt and ground black pepper to taste

## Instructions

1. Take a baking dish and grease it with the organic ghee.
2. Whisk the eggs with a pinch of salt in a deep bowl.
3. Pour the milk and continue to whisk.
4. Add all remaining ingredients one by one.
5. When all the ingredients are thoroughly blended, pour all of it into the prepared baking dish.
6. Add 1 cup water to the inner stainless steel pot in the Instant Pot, and place the trivet inside.
7. Place the baking dish on a trivet.
8. Lock lid into place and set on the MANUAL setting for 30 minutes.
9. When the timer beeps, press "Cancel" and carefully flip the Quick Release valve to let the pressure out.

10. Serve warm.

**Servings:** 8

**Cooking Times**

Total Time: 50 minutes

**Nutrition Facts**

Serving size: 1/8 of a recipe (6.5 ounces)

Percent daily values based on the Reference Daily Intake (RDI) for a 2000 calorie diet.

Nutrition information calculated from recipe ingredients.

**Amount Per Serving**

Calories 168,89

Calories From Fat (53%) 89,15

**% Daily Value**

Total Fat 9,91g 15%

Saturated Fat 3,52g 18%

Cholesterol 352,41mg 117%

Sodium 253,29mg 11%

Potassium 297,53mg 9%

Total Carbohydrates 5,43g 2%

Fiber 0,56g 2%

Sugar 3,58g

Protein 14,07g 28%

# Light Vegetable Breakfast Cake (Instant Pot)

## Ingredients

- 6 large eggs organic
- 1/2 cup milk
- 1/2 tsp salt and ground black pepper

- 2 Tbs chives chopped
- 1 cup Cheddar cheese shredded
- 1 cup water

## Instructions

1. Line a cake pan with aluminum foil. Coat inside of the pan with oil or nonstick spray.
2. Whisk together the eggs, milk, chives, salt, and pepper in a bowl.
3. Layer the cheese into the cake pan, then pour the egg mixture over the top.
4. Pour the water into your Instant Pot and place a metal trivet.
5. Place the baking pan on a trivet.
6. Lock the lid in place and select MANUAL, and set time for 30 minutes, making sure the valve in the lid is closed.
7. When the pressure cooker beeps, use a Quick pressure release.
8. Carefully open the lid, remove the pan, and let cool slightly before slicing.
9. Slice and serve.

**Servings:** 4

**Cooking Times**

Total Time: 40 minutes

**Nutrition Facts**

Serving size: 1/4 of a recipe (7 ounces)

Percent daily values based on the Reference Daily Intake (RDI) for a 2000 calorie diet. Nutrition information calculated from recipe ingredients.

**Amount Per Serving**

Calories 236,8

Calories From Fat (64%) 152,13

**% Daily Value**

Total Fat 17,11g 26%

Saturated Fat 8,69g 43%

Cholesterol 311,1mg 104%

Sodium 298,09mg 12%

Potassium 178,92mg 5%

Total Carbohydrates 2,43g <1%

Fiber 0,04g <1%

Sugar 2g

Protein 17,51g 35%

# Mushroom Omelette with Pecorino Romano (Instant Pot)

## Ingredients

- 8 large eggs, at room temperature
- 1 1/2 cup Portabella mushrooms cleaned, sliced
- 1/4 cup Pecorino Romano cheese freshly grated
- 2 Tbsp olive oil
- salt and ground white pepper to taste
- 1 cup water

## Instructions

1. Whisk the eggs with salt and pepper until set.
2. Add sliced mushrooms and Pecorino Romano cheese; stir well.
3. Grease the heat-proof baking dish and pour the egg mixture.
4. Pour one cup of water and place the trivet in your Instant Pot.
5. Place the baking dish on the top of the trivet.
6. Lock lid into place and set on the STEAM setting for 10 minutes.
7. After the pressure cooking time has finished use Quick Release - turn the valve from sealing to venting to release the pressure.
8. Carefully open the lid and transfer omelet to a serving platter.
9. Serve hot.

**Servings:** 4

**Cooking Times**

Total Time: 20 minutes

**Nutrition Facts**

Serving size: 1/4 of a recipe (5.5 ounces)

Percent daily values based on the Reference Daily Intake (RDI) for a 2000 calorie diet.

Nutrition information calculated from recipe ingredients.

**Amount Per Serving**

Calories 170,81

Calories From Fat (62%) 106,57

**% Daily Value**

Total Fat 11,88g 18%

Saturated Fat 3,45g 17%

Cholesterol 372mg 124%

Sodium 289,19mg 12%

Potassium 252,53mg 7%

Total Carbohydrates 1,89g <1%

Fiber 0,36g 1%

Sugar 1,08g

Protein 13,67g 27%

# Olives and Sun-dried Tomato Bread (Instant Pot)

## Ingredients

- 3/4 cup all-purpose flour
- 1/2 cup black olives chopped
- 1/2 cup Sun-dried tomatoes, finely chopped
- 1 onion finely chopped
- 1 Tbs oregano freshly chopped
- 1/2 cup yogurt

- 1/3 cup olive oil
- 3 eggs
- 1/4 cup Gruyere cheese
- 1 Tbs of powdered yeast
- Salt and ground black pepper
- 1 cup water for Instant Pot

## Instructions

1. In a large bowl, mix the flour, yeast, oregano, salt, and pepper, olives, tomato, onion and cheese.
2. Whisk the eggs with yogurt and olive oil in a separate bowl.
3. Combine the flour mixture with egg mixture and stir well.
4. Grease a baking dish and pour the batter.
5. Add water to the inner stainless steel pot in the Instant Pot, and place the trivet inside.
6. Place a baking dish on a trivet.
7. Lock lid into place and set on the MANUAL setting for 30 minutes.
8. When the timer beeps, press "Cancel" and carefully flip the Quick Release valve to let the pressure out.
9. Let cook for 10 - 15 minutes, slice and serve.

**Servings:** 8

**Cooking Times**

Total Time: 50 minutesž

**Nutrition Facts**

Serving size: 1/8 of a recipe (3,4 ounces).

Percent daily values based on the Reference Daily Intake (RDI) for a 2000 calorie diet.

Nutrition information calculated from recipe ingredients.

**Amount Per Serving**

Calories 201,51

Calories From Fat (61%) 122,66

**% Daily Value**

Total Fat 13,96g 21%

Saturated Fat 2,72g 14%

Cholesterol 73,31mg 24%

Sodium 156,32mg 7%

Potassium 258,12mg 7%

Total Carbohydrates 13,98g 5%

Fiber 2,77g 11%

Sugar 1,91g

Protein 6,88g 14%

# Popeye Cream Breakfast (Instant Pot)

## Ingredients

- 2 Tbsp extra virgin olive oil
- 1 small onion, chopped
- 1 lb baby spinach leaves
- 1/2 lb Kale

- 2 cups water
- 1 1/4 cups full fat milk
- Sea salt and black ground pepper to taste

## Instructions

1. Wash the vegetables and cut it into thick slices.
2. Press SAUTÉ button on your Instant Pot and heat the oil.
3. Sauté the onion with a pinch of salt for 2 - 3 minutes or until softened.
4. Add spinach and kale and sauté for 2 - 3 minutes.
5. Pour the water and season salt and pepper; stir well.
6. Lock lid into place and set on the MANUAL setting for 5 minutes.
7. When the timer beeps, press "Cancel" and carefully flip the Quick Release valve to let the pressure out.
8. Transfer the mixture to your blender and pour the milk; blend until creamy.
9. Taste and adjust salt and pepper to taste.
10. Pour into bowls and serve.

**Servings:** 6

**Cooking Times**

Total Time: 20 minutes

**Nutrition Facts**

Serving size: 1/6 of a recipe (7 ounces)

Percent daily values based on the Reference Daily Intake (RDI) for a 2000 calorie diet.

Nutrition information calculated from recipe ingredients.

**Amount Per Serving**

Calories 92,31

Calories From Fat (55%) 51,22

**% Daily Value**

Total Fat 5,79g 9%

Saturated Fat 1,3g 7%

Cholesterol 4,08mg 1%

Sodium 43,5mg 2%

Potassium 271,03mg 8%

Total Carbohydrates 8,14g 3%

Fiber 1,11g 4%                    Protein 3,15g 6%

Sugar 3,44g

# Porridge with Pumpkin Seeds and Berries (Instant Pot)

## Ingredients

- 1/4 cup ground flaxseed
- 1/4 cup oatmeal
- 1 cup full-fat milk
- **Toppings**
- 1 cup berries (any type)
- 2 Tbs coconut shaved

- 1 tsp pure vanilla extract
- 1 tsp cinnamon
- palm sugar to taste (optional)

- 2 Tbs pumpkin seeds

## Instructions

1. Place ground flaxseed, almond flour, milk, vanilla extract, cinnamon and palm sugar (if used) in your Instant Pot.
2. Lock lid into place and set on the PORRIDGE setting for 20 minutes.
3. When the timer beeps, press "Cancel" and carefully flip the Quick Release valve to let the pressure out.
4. Let cool for 10 minutes and pour the porridge into serving bowls.
5. Decorate with fresh berries, pumpkin seeds and shaved coconut. Serve.

**Servings:** 4

**Cooking Times**

Total Time: 30 minutes

**Nutrition Facts**

Serving size: 1/4 of a recipe (5 ounces)

Percent daily values based on the Reference Daily Intake (RDI) for a 2000 calorie diet.

Nutrition information calculated from recipe ingredients.

**Amount Per Serving**

Calories 111,48

Calories From Fat (25%) 27,77

**% Daily Value**

| | |
|---|---|
| Total Fat 3,23g 5% | Total Carbohydrates 16,75g 6% |
| Saturated Fat 1,71g 9% | Fiber 2,84g 11% |
| Cholesterol 4,88mg 2% | Sugar 7g |
| Sodium 80,69mg 3% | Protein 4,41g 9% |
| Potassium 186,77mg 5% | |

# Savory Oat Porridge with Vegetables (Instant Pot)

## Ingredients

- 1 cup vegetable broth
- 1/4 cup oatmeal

- 1 carrot sliced
- 1 potato sliced

- 1 tsp sunflower seeds
- 1 tsp fresh thyme
- salt and ground pepper to taste

## Instructions

1. Pour the vegetable broth, carrots, potatoes to Instant Pot's inner pot.
2. Lock lid into place and set on the MANUAL setting for 20 minutes.
3. Use Quick Release - turn the valve from sealing to venting to release the pressure.
4. Taste and adjust salt and pepper (if needed).
5. Sprinkle the porridge with sunflower seeds, garnish with thyme and serve.

**Servings:** 3

**Cooking Times**

Total Time: 25 minutes

**Nutrition Facts**

Serving size: 1/3 of a recipe (6.5 ounces)

Percent daily values based on the Reference Daily Intake (RDI) for a 2000 calorie diet.

Nutrition information calculated from recipe ingredients.

**Amount Per Serving**

Calories 143,42

Calories From Fat (14%) 19,83

**% Daily Value**

Total Fat 2,28g 4%

Saturated Fat 0,44g 2%

Cholesterol 0,82mg <1%

Sodium 762,16mg 32%

Potassium 506,87mg 14%

Total Carbohydrates 26,92g 9%

Fiber 3,97g 16%

Sugar 1,85g

Protein 4,55g 9%

# <u>L U N C H</u>

## Chaomi Rice with Tamari Sauce (Instant Pot)

### Ingredients

- 2 Tbsp garlic infused olive oil
- 2 scallion, chopped
- 1 cup of brown rice
- 1 1/2 cup of water
- 2 Tbsp tamari (or soy sauce)
- 2 piece Salt and black ground pepper to taste

### Instructions

1. Press SAUTÉ button on your Instant Pot and heat the oil.
2. Sauté a scallion with a pinch of salt for 4 minutes.
3. Add the rice and all remaining ingredients to Instant Pot's inner pot/liner.
4. Lock lid into place and set on the RICE setting for 3 minutes.
5. After the pressure cooking time has finished, use Natural Release - it takes 10 - 25 minutes to depressurize naturally.
6. Taste and adjust seasonings to taste.
7. Serve warm.

**Servings:** 4

**Cooking Times**

Total Time: 15 minutes

**Nutrition Facts**

Serving size: 1/4 of a recipe (8 ounces)

Percent daily values based on the Reference Daily Intake (RDI) for a 2000 calorie diet.

Nutrition information calculated from recipe ingredients.

**Amount Per Serving**

Calories 207,67

Calories From Fat (6%) 13,18

**% Daily Value**

Total Fat 1,6g 2%

Saturated Fat 0,03g <1%

Cholesterol 0mg 0%

Sodium 508,74mg 21%

Potassium 130,26mg 4%

Total Carbohydrates 47,95g 16%

Fiber 4,22g 17%

Sugar 2,8g

Protein 4,95g 10%

# Chilly Red Potato Salad with Mayonnaise (Instant Pot)

## Ingredients

- 6 medium red potatoes (scrubbed)
- 1 cup water

- 1 cup  mayonnaise
- 1 tsp Stone-ground mustard

- 1 tsp lemon juice freshly squeezed
- 1 cup onion finely chopped
- 2 Tbs  fresh dill, chopped
- 1 stalk celery (chopped)
- salt and pepper to taste

## Instructions

1. Wash and scrub the potatoes.
2. Place the potatoes in Instant Pot's inner pot/liner.
3. Salt to the potatoes and pour the water to cover potatoes.
4. Cover the pot and make sure the vent is set to "seal."
5. Lock lid into place and set on the MANUAL setting for 8 minutes.
6. Use Quick Release - turn the valve from sealing to venting to release the pressure.
7. Peel and dice potatoes once they are cool enough to handle.
8. Place the potatoes in a shallow bowl.
9. Combine the mayo, mustard, lemon juice, chopped onion, celery and dill in a bowl.
10. Add the mayo mixture to the potatoes and gently stir with wooden spoon.
11. Chill at least one hour before serving.

**Servings:** 4

**Cooking Times**

Total Time: 20 minutes

**Nutrition Facts**

Serving size: 1/4 of a recipe (10 ounces)

Percent daily values based on the Reference Daily Intake (RDI) for a 2000 calorie diet.

Nutrition information calculated from recipe ingredients.

**Amount Per Serving**

Calories 255,62

Calories From Fat (36%) 92

**% Daily Value**

Total Fat 10,19g 16%

Saturated Fat 1,54g 8%

Cholesterol 10,5mg 4%

Sodium 278,81mg 12%

Potassium 1107,65mg 32%

Sugar 1,91g

Total Carbohydrates 37,65g 13%

Protein 4,51g 9%

Fiber 3,56g 14%

# Creamy Sweet Potatoes Mash (Instant Pot)

## Ingredients

- 2 lb sweet potatoes peeled
- 2 Tbs butter grass-fed
- 1/2 cup fresh cream

- 1/3 tsp cinnamon
- Sea salt to taste

## Instructions

1. Rinse the potatoes thoroughly to wash away any dirt.
2. Place sweet potato chunks in your Instant Pot with a butter and a pinch of salt.
3. Lock lid into place, set on "Steam" program and set time for 10 minutes.
4. Use Quick Release - turn the valve from sealing to venting to release the pressure.
5. Transfer the potatoes in a blender, add salt to taste, some more butter, cream, and cinnamon.
6. Blend until creamy and serve immediately.

**Servings**: 4

**Cooking Times**

Total Time: 20 minutes

**Nutrition Facts**

Serving size: 1/4 of a recipe (9.5 ounces)

Percent daily values based on the Reference Daily Intake (RDI) for a 2000 calorie diet.

Nutrition information calculated from recipe ingredients.

**Amount Per Serving**

Calories 315,09

Calories From Fat (35%) 111,39

**% Daily Value**

Total Fat 13,02g 20%

Saturated Fat 10,02g 50%

Cholesterol 15,27mg 5%

Sodium 130,02mg 5%

Potassium 845,19mg 24%

Total Carbohydrates 47,36g 16%

Fiber 7,51g 30%

Sugar 10,49g

Protein 4,31g 9%

# Delicious Creamy Tomato Soup (Instant Pot)

## Ingredients

- 1/4 cup of olive oil
- 1/4 cup green onion, finely chopped
- 2 cloves garlic finely chopped
- 1/2 cup Sun-dried Tomatoes

- 1 1/2 lb fresh tomatoes in cubes
- 1 1/2 cup water
- 1 glass red wine
- 3 tsp Apple cider vinegar
- 1 bunch of basil, finely chopped
- Salt and ground pepper
- 1/2 tsp paprika sweet, powder
- 1 cup milk full fat

## Instructions

1. Press SAUTÉ button on your Instant Pot and heat the oil.
2. Sauté green onions and sun-dried tomatoes for 3 minutes.
3. Add the fresh tomatoes, 1/2 cup water, vinegar, wine and half basil.
4. Season salt the pepper, add the sweet paprika and simmer for 2 minutes.
5. Lock lid into place and set on the MANUAL setting for 5 minutes.
6. Use Natural Release - it takes 10 - 25 minutes to depressurize naturally.
7. Transfer the tomato soup to your fast-speed blender.
8. Pour the milk and blend until smooth and creamy.
9. Taste and adjust salt and pepper.
10. Serve warm.

**Servings:** 6

**Cooking Times**

Total Time: 35 minutes

**Nutrition Facts**

Serving size: 1/6 of a recipe (8.5 ounces)

Percent daily values based on the Reference Daily Intake (RDI) for a 2000 calorie diet.

Nutrition information calculated from recipe ingredients.

**Amount Per Serving**

Calories 176,29

Calories From Fat (72%) 126,26

% Daily Value

Total Fat 14,58g 22%

Saturated Fat 5,03g 25%

Cholesterol 0mg 0%

Sodium 36,68mg 2%

Potassium 513,19mg 15%

Total Carbohydrates 8,54g 3%

Fiber 2,3g 9%

Sugar 3,22g

Protein 2,17g 4%

# Fava and Mushrooms with Wine Stew (Instant Pot)

## Ingredients

- 3 Tbsp Olive oil
- 1 medium onion finely chopped
- 2 lbs fresh fava beans in the pod
- 3 cups water

- 1 lb mushroom blend (ready to eat)
- 1/2 tsp Salt and fresh-ground black pepper to taste
- 1/2 cup white wine

## Instructions

1. Remove fava beans from pods and rinse under cold running water; set aside.
2. Press SAUTÉ button on your Instant Pot and heat the oil.
3. Sauté the onion until soft, for 2 - 3 minutes.
4. Add the fava beans; secure the lid on the Instant Pot, turning the valve to "Sealing".
5. Select the Bean / Chili cycle and select 25 - 30 minutes.
6. When the timer beeps, allow for a natural release for 15 minutes, then do a quick release.
7. Add mushrooms, wine, salt, and pepper to taste in a bowl.
8. Combine the fava with mushrooms mixture and gently stir.
9. Ready! Serve and enjoy!

**Servings:** 6

**Cooking Times**

Total Time: 50 minutes

**Nutrition Facts**

Serving size: 1/6 of a recipe (10 ounces)

Percent daily values based on the Reference Daily Intake (RDI) for a 2000 calorie diet.

Nutrition information calculated from recipe ingredients.

**Amount Per Serving**

Calories 233,63

Calories From Fat (30%) 69,66

**% Daily Value**

| | |
|---|---|
| Total Fat 7,95g 12% | Total Carbohydrates 32,32g 11% |
| Saturated Fat 1,13g 6% | Fiber 0,8g 3% |
| Cholesterol 0mg 0% | Sugar 2,35g |
| Sodium 92,72mg 4% | Protein 14,1g 28% |
| Potassium 884,46mg 25% | |

# Full Protein Quinoa Pilaf (Instant Pot)

## Ingredients

- 1/4 cup olive oil
- 1/2 onion, chopped
- 2 cloves garlic (finely chopped fresh)
- 1 carrot, chopped

- 1 tomato, chopped
- 2 cup quinoa
- 1 1/2 cup broccoli florets, cut into small pieces
- 1/4 cup peas
- 3 cups vegetable broth
- 2 cups water
- 1 tsp ground black pepper
- 1 tsp thyme

## Instructions

1. Press SAUTÉ button on your Instant Pot and heat the oil.
2. Sauté the onion and garlic with a pinch of salt for 2 - 3 minutes, Add the quinoa, water and broth; season thyme and salt and pepper.
3. Add the carrots and peas; stir. Finally, add the tomatoes and broccoli; stir.
4. Select "Manual" mode and press the "-" button until it reads 10 minutes.
5. When the timer beeps, press "Cancel" and carefully flip the Quick Release valve to let the pressure out.
6. Taste and adjust seasonings to taste.
7. Serve hot.

**Servings:** 6

**Cooking Times**

Total Time: 25 minutes

**Nutrition Facts**

Serving size: 1/6 of a recipe (11,9 ounces).

Percent daily values based on the Reference Daily Intake (RDI) for a 2000 calorie diet.

Nutrition information calculated from recipe ingredients.

**Amount Per Serving**

Calories 395,21

Calories From Fat (33%) 129,36

**% Daily Value**

Total Fat 14,56g 22%                    Saturated Fat 2,12g 11%

Cholesterol 1,23mg <1%

Sodium 840,44mg 35%

Potassium 701,2mg 20%

Total Carbohydrates 55,03g 18%

Fiber 6,83g 27%

Sugar 1,96g

Protein 12,35g 25%

# Italian Vegetable Soup with Rice (Instant Pot)

## Ingredients

- 1 cup olive oil
- 4 green onions (white and green parts), chopped
- 10 oz fresh spinach
- 3 crushed garlic cloves
- 2 carrots sliced
- 1 cup rice (cooked)
- 2 potatoes sliced
- 3 cups vegetable broth (Gluten-free)
- 2 cups water
- 1 cup celery (chopped)
- 1 cup parsley (chopped)
- 2 Tbsp fresh lemon juice
- 3 Tbsp tomato paste
- 1/2 cup parmesan cheese (grated)
- 1 bay leaf
- 1 tsp Salt and black pepper to taste
- 2 tsp dried basil

## Instructions

1. Press SAUTÉ button on your Instant Pot and heat the olive oil. Sauté the onions, garlic, and carrots for 3 minutes; stir.

2. Add the rice and potatoes; season salt an pepper and stir well.
3. Pour the broth, water, celery, parsley, bay leaf, pepper, basil, tomato paste and lemon juice; stir well.
4. Lock lid into place and set on the MANUAL setting for 10 minutes.
5. Use Natural Release - it takes 10 - 25 minutes to depressurize naturally.
6. Open the lid, taste and adjust seasonings to taste.
7. Ladle soup into bowls. Sprinkle the Parmesan cheese and serve.

**Servings:** 8

**Cooking Times**

Total Time: 45 minutes

**Nutrition Facts**

Serving size: 1/8 of a recipe (10.5 ounces)

Percent daily values based on the Reference Daily Intake (RDI) for a 2000 calorie diet.

Nutrition information calculated from recipe ingredients.

**Amount Per Serving**

Calories 260,59

Calories From Fat (36%) 93,09

**% Daily Value**

Total Fat 10,56g 16%

Saturated Fat 2,42g 12%

Cholesterol 6,42mg 2%

Sodium 1187,23mg 49%

Potassium 671,06mg 19%

Total Carbohydrates 34,48g 11%

Fiber 4,96g 20%

Sugar 2,77g

Protein 8,72g 17%

# Mediterranean Creamy Carrot Soup (Instant Pot)

## Ingredients

- ¼ cup Garlic-infused Olive oil
- 1 cup scallion finely chopped
- 1 1/2 lb carrot sliced
- 2 cups water
- 2 cups vegetable broth (gluten free)

- 1 Tbsp  fresh dill, chopped
- 1 Tbsp  fresh sage, chopped
- Salt and pepper to taste
- 3/4 cup fresh cream

## Instructions

1. Press SAUTÉ button on your Instant Pot and heat garlic-infused olive oil.
2. Sauté the scallions and carrots with a little salt.
3. Pour the water and the broth, and add all remaining ingredients (except the cream); simmer for 2-3 minutes and stir.
4. Select "Manual" mode and press the "-" button until it reads 10 minutes. Also, make sure to set the top knob to "Sealing" and not "Venting".
5. When the timer beeps, press "Cancel" and carefully flip the Quick Release valve to let the pressure out.
6. Transfer your soup to a blender, add the fresh cream and blend until creamy and soft.
7. Taste and adjust seasonings.
8. Serve immediately.

**Servings:** 6

**Cooking Times**

Total Time: 25 minutes

**Nutrition Facts**

Serving size: 1/6 of a recipe (11 ounces)

Percent daily values based on the Reference Daily Intake (RDI) for a 2000 calorie diet.

Nutrition information calculated from recipe ingredients.

**Amount Per Serving**

Calories 210,24

Calories From Fat (53%) 110,87

**% Daily Value**

| | |
|---|---|
| Total Fat 12,6g 19% | Total Carbohydrates 22,03g 7% |
| Saturated Fat 7,19g 36% | Fiber 4,69g 19% |
| Cholesterol 41,58mg 14% | Sugar 5,81g |
| Sodium 733,71mg 31% | Protein 4,02g 8% |
| Potassium 565,71mg 16% | |

# Minestrone Tortellini with Parmesan Cheese (Instant Pot)

## Ingredients

- 2 Tbs olive oil
- 1 large onion, diced
- 1 Tbs fresh garlic, minced
- 2 stalks celery, sliced
- 2 carrots, sliced
- 8 oz dry tortellini
- 3 cups vegetable broth

- 1 cup water
- 1 can (15 oz) spaghetti sauce
- 1 can (15 oz) diced tomatoes
- 1 1/2 tsp Italian seasoning
- 1/4 tsp Salt and black pepper or to taste
- 1/4 cup Parmesan cheese freshly grated

## Instructions

1. Press SAUTÉ button on your Instant Pot and heat the oil.
2. Sauté the onion, garlic, carrots, and celery for 3 - 4 minutes.
3. Add all remaining ingredients and stir to combine well.
4. Select "Manual" mode and press the "-" button until it reads 6 minutes. Also, make sure to set the top knob to "Sealing" and not "Venting".
5. When the timer beeps, press "Cancel" and carefully flip the Quick Release valve to let the pressure out.
6. Serve with shredded Parmesan cheese.

**Servings:** 6

**Cooking Times**

Total Time: 15 minutes

**Nutrition Facts**

Serving size: 1/6 of a recipe (12 ounces)

Percent daily values based on the Reference Daily Intake (RDI) for a 2000 calorie diet.

Nutrition information calculated from recipe ingredients.

**Amount Per Serving**

Calories 306,57

Calories From Fat (34%) 103,05

**% Daily Value**

| | |
|---|---|
| Total Fat 11,54g 18% | Total Carbohydrates 39,7g 13% |
| Saturated Fat 3,07g 15% | Fiber 5,33g 21% |
| Cholesterol 31,91mg 11% | Sugar 5,92g |
| Sodium 1382,3mg 58% | Protein 11,77g 24% |
| Potassium 549,2mg 16% | |

# Mustard Greens Sour "Stew" (Instant Pot)

## Ingredients

- 2 Tbsp olive oil
- 1 green onion finely sliced

- 3 cloves minced garlic (can use more or less)
- 1 lb fresh Mustard greens
- 1/2 cup water
- 2 Tbsp tomato puree
- 3 tsp lemon juice freshly squeezed
- 1/2 tsp salt
- 1 tsp sugar

## Instructions

1. Wash and clean well the mustard greens leaves. Remove the thickest parts of the stems at the base of greens. Chop the stems into small pieces.
2. Press SAUTÉ button on your Instant Pot and heat the oil.
3. Saute the green onion and garlic with a pinch of salt for 2 - 3 minutes.
4. Add the mustard greens and saute, stirring occasionally, for 2 minutes.
5. Add all remaining ingredients, season salt, and pepper.
6. Lock lid into place and set on the MANUAL setting for 12 minutes.
7. Use Quick Release - turn the valve from sealing to venting to release the pressure.
8. Taste and adjust seasonings to taste.
9. Serve with extra lemon juice.

**Servings:** 4

**Cooking Times**

Total Time: 30 minutes

**Nutrition Facts**

Serving size: 1/4 of a recipe (7 ounces)

Percent daily values based on the Reference Daily Intake (RDI) for a 2000 calorie diet.

Nutrition information calculated from recipe ingredients.

**Amount Per Serving**

Calories 115,44

Calories From Fat (56%) 64,19

**% Daily Value**

Total Fat 7,29g 11%                    Saturated Fat 1,01g 5%

Cholesterol 0mg 0%

Sodium 326,77mg 14%

Potassium 263,76mg 8%

Total Carbohydrates 11,66g 4%

Fiber 4,74g 19%

Sugar 3,16g

Protein 3,33g 7%

# Red Beans and Mushroom Stew (Instant Pot)

## Ingredients

- 1/4 cup Olive oil
- 1 onion, chopped
- 2 -3 tsp garlic
- 2 cups button mushrooms, chopped
- 2 cups  crushed tomatoes

- 2 carrots, chopped
- 2 cups red beans, drained & rinsed
- 1 tsp red chili pepper (chopped)
- 1 tsp dried oregano
- 2 cups vegetable stock

## Instructions

1. Press SAUTÉ button on your Instant Pot and heat the oil.
2. Sauté the onion, garlic with a little salt for 2 - 3 minutes.
3. Add the mushrooms and carrots and sauté for 2 minutes; stir.
4. Add all remaining ingredients and stir well.
5. Lock lid into place and set on the MANUAL setting for 10 minutes.
6. Use Quick Release - turn the valve from sealing to venting to release the pressure.
7. Taste and adjust seasonings to taste.

8. Serve hot.

**Servings:** 8

**Cooking Times**

Preparation Time: 35 minutes

Total Time: 25 minutes

**Nutrition Facts**

Serving size: 1/8 of a recipe (11.5 ounces)

Percent daily values based on the Reference Daily Intake (RDI) for a 2000 calorie diet.

Nutrition information calculated from recipe ingredients.

**Amount Per Serving**

Calories 251,86

Calories From Fat (31%) 78,62

**% Daily Value**

Total Fat 8,92g 14%

Saturated Fat 0,94g 5%

Cholesterol 1,24mg <1%

Sodium 904,27mg 38%

Potassium 667,16mg 19%

Total Carbohydrates 35,24g 12%

Fiber 9,06g 36%

Sugar 6,01g

Protein 10,04g 20%

# Spicy Brussels sprouts with Siracha Sauce

## Ingredients

- 2 lb Brussels sprouts halved
- 2 Tbs Sriracha sauce
- 1/4 cup soy sauce gluten free
- 3 Tbs sesame oil
- 1 Tbs chopped almonds
- 1/2 Tbs cayenne pepper

- 1 tsp red pepper flakes
- 1 Tbs smoked paprika
- 2 tsp garlic powder
- 1 tsp onion powder
- Salt and pepper to taste

## Instructions

1. Put Brussels sprouts in your Instant Pot and add sriracha sauce and soy sauce.
2. Add all ingredients and pour water; stir.
3. Lock lid into place and set on the MANUAL setting for 3 minutes.
4. When the timer beeps, press "Cancel" and carefully flip the Quick Release valve to let the pressure out.
5. Taste and adjust seasonings to taste.
6. Serve immediately.

**Servings:** 4

## Cooking Times

Total Time: 10 minutes

## Nutrition Facts

Serving size: 1/4 of a recipe (10 ounces)

Percent daily values based on the Reference Daily Intake (RDI) for a 2000 calorie diet.

Nutrition information calculated from recipe ingredients.

## Amount Per Serving

Calories 227,05

Calories From Fat (47%) 107,78

## % Daily Value

Total Fat 12,3g 19%

Saturated Fat 1,73g 9%

Cholesterol 0mg 0%

Sodium 1238,64mg 52%

Potassium 1013,1mg 29%

Total Carbohydrates 25,26g 8%

Fiber 9,94g 40%

Sugar 5,8g

Protein 10,48g 21%

# Spinach Puree with Almonds (Instant Pot)

## Ingredients

- 1/4 cup Garlic infused virgin olive oil
- 1 onion finely chopped
- 1 1/2 lb baby spinach leaves
- 2 cups water
- 1 cup vegetable broth
- 1 small turnip chopped

- salt and black ground pepper to taste
- 1/2 cup walnuts chopped

## Instructions

1. Peel the turnip and cut it into small pieces. Wash the leek and cut it into thick slices.
2. Press SAUTÉ button on your Instant Pot and sauté onion with a pinch of salt for 2-3 minutes.
3. Add the spinach leaves, water, broth and season salt and pepper to taste; stir and sauté for one minute.
4. Add the turnip and sauté for 2 minutes more; stir well.
5. Lock lid into place and set on the MANUAL setting for 5 minutes.
6. Use Quick Release - turn the valve from sealing to venting to release the pressure.
7. Carefully open the lid and transfer the vegetables to a blender. Blend into a very smooth soup.
8. Pour the soup into bowls and sprinkle with ground toasted almonds.
9. Serve.

**Servings:** 6

**Cooking Times**

Total Time: 25 minutes

**Nutrition Facts**

Serving size: 1/6 of a recipe (7 ounces)

Percent daily values based on the Reference Daily Intake (RDI) for a 2000 calorie diet.

Nutrition information calculated from recipe ingredients.

**Amount Per Serving**

Calories 127,15

Calories From Fat (69%) 87,97

**% Daily Value**

| | |
|---|---|
| Total Fat 9,96g 15% | Sodium 393,98mg 16% |
| Saturated Fat 1,42g 7% | Potassium 154,19mg 4% |
| Cholesterol 0,42mg <1% | Total Carbohydrates 8,57g 3% |

Fiber 1,41g 6%

Sugar 1,76g

Protein 1,6g 3%

# Tasty Corn Soup (Instant Pot)

## Ingredients

- 2 Tbs butter grass-fed, unsalted
- 1 1/2 cups leeks, chopped
- 6 ears of corn, kernels
- 2 cloves garlic, thinly sliced
- 1/4 tsp fennel seed
- 2 bay leaves

- 3 cups vegetable broth
- 1 cup water
- Salt and freshly ground black pepper to taste
- 2 Tbsp Extra-virgin olive oil, for serving
- crouton

## Instructions

1. Press SAUTÉ button on your Instant and sauté the leeks and garlic with a little salt about 4 minutes; stir.
2. Add the corn with cobs, fennel seed, bay leaves and pour broth and water; stir to combine.
3. Lock lid into place and set on the MANUAL setting for 5 minutes.
4. After the pressure cooking time has finished using Natural Release - it takes 10 - 25 minutes to depressurize naturally.
5. Remove the lid and transfer the corn mixture to the blender.
6. Blend on SLOW and gradually increase speed to HIGH until completely soft.
7. Taste and adjust salt and pepper to taste.

8. Serve with a splash of olive oil and croutons.

**Servings:** 6

**Cooking Times**

Preparation Time: 25 minutes

**Nutrition Facts**

Serving size: 1/6 of a recipe (10.5 ounces)

Percent daily values based on the Reference Daily Intake (RDI) for a 2000 calorie diet.

Nutrition information calculated from recipe ingredients.

**Amount Per Serving**

Calories 231,63

Calories From Fat (26%) 59,32

**% Daily Value**

| | |
|---|---|
| Total Fat 6,76g 10% | Total Carbohydrates 40,34g 13% |
| Saturated Fat 3,03g 15% | Fiber 4,74g 19% |
| Cholesterol 11,41mg 4% | Sugar 0,88g |
| Sodium 927,87mg 39% | Protein 6,87g 14% |
| Potassium 471,42mg 13% | |

# Zucchini Noodles with Goat Cheese (Instant Pot)

## Ingredients

- 1/4 cup Extra virgin olive oil
- 2 cloves mashed garlic
- 3 cups zucchini noodles (zoodles)
- Salt and fresh cracked pepper to taste
- 3 Tbsp fresh basil (chopped)
- 1/2 cup goat cheese crumbled
- 1 tsp red pepper flakes
- 1 Tbsp chopped red pepper
- 1 cup vegetable broth

## Instructions

1. Wash and clean zucchini and peel into long strips.
2. Press SAUTÉ button on your Instant Pot and heat the olive oil.
3. Sauté the garlic for 2-3 minutes.
4. Add zucchini strips and cook for 2 minutes.
5. Season salt and pepper, chopped basil, red pepper flakes, chopped red pepper.
6. Pour the vegetable broth and stir well.
7. Lock lid into place and set on the MANUAL setting for 3 minutes.
8. Use Quick Release - turn the valve from sealing to venting to release the pressure.
9. Sprinkle with goat crumbled cheese and serve hot.

**Servings:** 4

**Cooking Times**

Total Time: 20 minutes

**Nutrition Facts**

Serving size: 1/4 of a recipe (9.5 ounces)

Percent daily values based on the Reference Daily Intake (RDI) for a 2000 calorie diet.

Nutrition information calculated from recipe ingredients.

**Amount Per Serving**

Calories 296,76

Calories From Fat (65%) 193,37

**% Daily Value**

Total Fat 21,94g 34%

Saturated Fat 6,56g 33%

Cholesterol 26,62mg 9%

Sodium 859,29mg 36%

Potassium 900,39mg 26%

Total Carbohydrates 13,9g 5%

Fiber 3,77g 15%

Sugar 0,34g

Protein 14,3g 29%

# DINNER

## "Baked" Okra with Grated Tomatoes (Instant Pot)

### Ingredients

- 1/4 cup garlic infused olive oil
- 2 spring onions finely chopped
- 2 carrots sliced
- 4 ripe tomatoes grated
- 2 lbs of okra
- 1 cup water

- 1 tsp white vinegar
- 2 pinches Salt and ground black pepper
- 1 tsp Chopped fresh parsley
- 1/4 cup grated Feta for serving (optional)

### Instructions

1. Wash and clean the okra.
2. Place okra in a deep bowl with a little vinegar and salt.
3. Press SAUTÉ button on your Instant Pot and heat the oil.
4. Saute the onions and chopped tomatoes with salt for 3 - 4 minutes; stir.
5. Add the okra and sliced carrots and cook, stirring, about 2-3 minutes.
6. Add all remaining ingredients (except Feta cheese).
7. Lock lid into place and set on the MANUAL setting for 4 minutes.
8. Naturally, release pressure for 5 minutes and quick release remaining pressure.

9.  Taste and adjust seasonings to taste.
10. Serve with a chopped parsley and grated feta cheese.

**Servings:** 6

**Cooking Times**

Total Time: 55 minutes

**Nutrition Facts**

Serving size: 1/6 of a recipe (11,5 ounces).

Percent daily values based on the Reference Daily Intake (RDI) for a 2000 calorie diet.

Nutrition information calculated from recipe ingredients.

**Amount Per Serving**

Calories 155,56

Calories From Fat (53%) 83

**% Daily Value**

Total Fat 9,41g 14%

Saturated Fat 1,32g 7%

Cholesterol 0mg 0%

Sodium 37,53mg 2%

Potassium 774,76mg 22%

Total Carbohydrates 17,16g 6%

Fiber 6,82g 27%

Sugar 5,58g

Protein 4,17g 8%

# "Grilled" Zucchini with Garlic and Herbs (Instant Pot)

## Ingredients

- 4 large zucchini
- 1/4 cup Olive oil
- Salt and ground black pepper to taste
- 1 tsp powdered garlic (or to taste)
- 1/2 tsp dry rosemary
- 1/2 tsp basil
- 1/4 tsp oregano
- 1 cup water
- 1/4 cup Parmesan cheese - grated

## Instructions

1. Cut the edges off zucchini and then cut them lengthwise.
2. With a brush, dip both sides with olive oil, salt the pepper, garlic and the herbs of your choice.
3. In the inner liner of your Instant Pot, place water and a steamer.
4. Place herbed zucchini on the seamer and lock lid into place.
5. Set in the MANUAL setting for 3 minutes.
6. When the timer beeps, press "Cancel" and carefully flip the Quick Release valve to let the pressure out.
7. Serve hot.

**Servings:** 4

**Cooking Times**

Total Time: 10 minutes

**Nutrition Facts**

Serving size: 1/4 of a recipe (10 ounces)

Percent daily values based on the Reference Daily Intake (RDI) for a 2000 calorie diet.

Nutrition information calculated from recipe ingredients.

**Amount Per Serving**

Calories 183,17

Calories From Fat (77%) 140,82

**% Daily Value**

Total Fat 15,97g 25%

Saturated Fat 3,13g 16%

Cholesterol 5,5mg 2%

Sodium 259,76mg 11%

Potassium 556,27mg 16%

Total Carbohydrates 7,07g 2%

Fiber 2,2g 9%

Sugar 5,23g

Protein 5g 10%

# Broad beans, Lentils and Peas Cream (Instant Pot)

## Ingredients

- 1/4 cup Olive oil
- 2 yellow onions, peeled and chopped
- 2 cloves garlic (finely chopped)
- Salt and freshly ground white pepper

- 1 lb broad beans (raw)
- 2 cups vegetable broth (fat-free)
- 1 cup peas, frozen and thawed
- 1 1/2 cups lentils, cooked and drained
- 4 cups water

## Instructions

1. Press SAUTÉ button on your Instant Pot and pour the oil.
2. Saute the onion and garlic with a pinch of salt for 3 - 4  minutes. Stir with a wooden spoon.
3. Add all remaining ingredients and stir well.
4. Turn off the saute mode.
5. Lock lid into place and set on the MANUAL setting for 55 - 60 minutes.
6. After the pressure cooking time has finished Naturally release pressure for 5 minutes and quick release remaining pressure.
7. Transfer bean and lentils mixture to the blender and blend until smooth and creamy.
8. Taste and adjust seasonings.
9. Let cool at room temperature or refrigerate for one hour.
10. Serve.

**Servings:** 8

**Cooking Times**

Total Time: 1 hour and 15 minutes

**Nutrition Facts**

Serving size: 1/8 of a recipe (10 ounces)

Percent daily values based on the Reference Daily Intake (RDI) for a 2000 calorie diet.

Nutrition information calculated from recipe ingredients.

**Amount Per Serving**

Calories 290,17

Calories From Fat (32%) 91,55

**% Daily Value**

Total Fat 10,33g 16%                    Saturated Fat 1,48g 7%

Cholesterol 0,9mg <1%

Sodium 156,42mg 7%

Potassium 622,37mg 18%

Total Carbohydrates 36,92g 12%

Fiber 12,12g 48%

Sugar 2,05g

Protein 15,66g 31%

## Brown Rice and Lentils with Cheddar Soup (Instant Pot)

## Ingredients

- 1/2 red onion finely chopped
- 1/2 red bell pepper finely chopped
- 4 garlic cloves minced
- 3/4 cup brown rice
- 3/4 cup brown lentils
- 1 1/2 cups vegetable broth
- 1 cup water
- 15 oz diced tomatoes

- 4 oz diced green chiles
- 1 Tbs taco seasoning
- 2 tsp dried oregano
- 1 tsp kosher salt and freshly ground black pepper
- 2 cups shredded Sharp Cheddar cheese
- 1/4 cup fresh cilantro chopped

## Instructions

1. Add all ingredients, (except cheese and cilantro), to your Instant Pot.
2. Stir well to combine all ingredients.
3. Lock lid into place and set on the MANUAL setting for 15 minutes.

4. After the pressure cooking time has finished using a Natural Release - it takes 10 - 25 minutes to depressurize naturally.
5. Transfer the mixture in a large serving dish and sprinkle with Cheddar cheese.
6. Let cool for 5 minutes.
7. Sprinkle with cilantro and serve.

**Servings:** 6

**Cooking Times**

Total Time: 40 minutes

**Nutrition Facts**

Serving size: 1/6 of a recipe (11 ounces)

Percent daily values based on the Reference Daily Intake (RDI) for a 2000 calorie diet.

Nutrition information calculated from recipe ingredients.

**Amount Per Serving**

Calories 428,86

Calories From Fat (36%) 154,21

**% Daily Value**

| | |
|---|---|
| Total Fat 17,13g 26% | Total Carbohydrates 50,43g 17% |
| Saturated Fat 6,46g 32% | Fiber 10,29g 41% |
| Cholesterol 30,86mg 10% | Sugar 2,55g |
| Sodium 1170,03mg 49% | Protein 17,99g 36% |
| Potassium 509,82mg 15% | |

# Chickpeas with Tomato, Mushrooms and Avocado Stew (Instant Pot)

## Instructions

- 1/2 cup virgin olive oil
- 8 whole cloves of garlic (or more)
- 2 can (15 oz) whole, peeled plum tomatoes
- 2 tsp smoked sweet paprika
- 1 cup fresh spinach (washed and chopped)

- 15 button mushrooms
- 2 can (15 oz) chickpeas
- 1/4 cup toasted pine nuts
- 1 avocado (fresh diced)
- Water

## Instructions

1. Press SAUTÉ button on your Instant Pot and pour the oil.
2. Sauté the garlic for 2 - 3 minutes.
3. Add the paprika and crushed tomatoes and stir well with a wooden spoon.
4. Add the spinach and add to a pot along with mushrooms.
5. Season salt and pepper to taste.
6. Drain and rinse the chickpeas and add to the Instant Pot.
7. Sauté for 5 minutes; stir occasionally.
8. Finally, add the avocado slices and pour the water.
9. Lock lid into place and set on the MANUAL setting for 20 minutes.
10. Use Natural Release - it takes 10 - 25 minutes to depressurize naturally.

11. Taste and adjust paprika, and salt and pepper to taste.

12. Serve sprinkled with pine nuts.

**Servings:** 6

**Cooking Times**

Total Time: 40 minutes

**Nutrition Facts**

Serving size: 1/6 of a recipe (11 ounces)

Percent daily values based on the Reference Daily Intake (RDI) for a 2000 calorie diet.

Nutrition information calculated from recipe ingredients.

**Amount Per Serving**

Calories 279,37

Calories From Fat (26%) 74,01

**% Daily Value**

Total Fat 8,84g 14%

Saturated Fat 0,98g 5%

Cholesterol 0mg 0%

Sodium 665,9mg 28%

Potassium 828,14mg 24%

Total Carbohydrates 41,64g 14%

Fiber 11,68g 47%

Sugar 1,75g

Protein 12,95g 26%

# Curried Carrots with Fresh Cream (Instant Pot)

## Ingredients

- 2 Tbs butter grass-fed
- 2 lbs carrots sliced
- 1 tsp curry powder
- 1/2 cup vegetable broth

- 1/2 cup water
- Seasoned salt and ground white pepper
- 1/2 cup Fresh cream
- 1 tsp Parsley chopped (for serving)

## Instructions

1. Peel the carrots and cut into thin slices.
2. Press SAUTÉ button on your Instant Pot.
3. Place the carrots and sauté with seasoned salt for 2 - 3 minutes.
4. Pour vegetable broth and water; stir.
5. Add curry powder and seasoned salt and pepper; stir.
6. Lock lid into place and set on the MANUAL setting for 10 minutes.
7. When the timer beeps, press "Cancel" and carefully flip the Quick Release valve to let the pressure out.
8. Carefully open the lid. Taste and adjust curry, salt, and pepper.
9. Add some cream, sprinkle with parsley and serve immediately.

**Servings**: 4

**Cooking Times**

Total Time: 20 minutes

**Nutrition Facts**

Serving size: 1/4 of a recipe (11 ounces)

Percent daily values based on the Reference Daily Intake (RDI) for a 2000 calorie diet.

Nutrition information calculated from recipe ingredients.

**Amount Per Serving**

Calories 269,6

Calories From Fat (58%) 156,9

**% Daily Value**

| | |
|---|---|
| Total Fat 17,87g 27% | Total Carbohydrates 26,4g 9% |
| Saturated Fat 10,71g 54% | Fiber 7,02g 28% |
| Cholesterol 56,33mg 19% | Sugar 10,8g |
| Sodium 373,18mg 16% | Protein 3,63g 7% |
| Potassium 808,07mg 23% | |

# Gourmet Fettuccine Alfredo (Instant Pot)

## Ingredients

- 6 egg yolks lightly beaten
- 1 cup Half and Half cream
- 2 Tbsp butter
- 2 cloves garlic (finely chopped fresh)

- 1 lb fettuccine
- black pepper freshly ground, to taste
- salt, to taste
- 1/2 cup Parmesan cheese freshly grated
- 2 cups water

## Instructions

1. In a medium bowl, blend the egg yolks and half-and-half cream together.
2. Press SAUTÉ button on your Instant Pot and heat the butter.
3. Sauté the garlic for 2 minutes with a pinch of salt (do not burn).
4. Add the egg/cream mixture and gently stir.
5. Add fettuccine and water, season with salt and pepper to taste.
6. Add grated Parmesan.
7. Turn off the Sauté mode. Seal the instant pot and set it to manual mode with 8 minutes cooking time.
8. When the timer beeps, press "Cancel" and carefully flip the Quick Release valve to let the pressure out.
9. Serve hot.

**Servings:** 6

**Nutrition Facts**

Serving size: 1/6 of a recipe (7 ounces)

Percent daily values based on the Reference Daily Intake (RDI) for a 2000 calorie diet.

Nutrition information calculated from recipe ingredients

**Amount Per Serving**

Calories 542,46

Calories From Fat (43%) 234,56

**% Daily Value**

Total Fat 26,51g 41%

Saturated Fat 14,77g 74%

Cholesterol 251,96mg 84%

Sodium 206,1mg 9%

Potassium 188,06mg 5%

Total Carbohydrates 58,92g 20%

Fiber 1,87g 7%

Sugar 0,23g

Protein 16,43g 33%

# Levantine Vegetarian Dish with Rice (Instant Pot)

## Ingredients

- 4 1/2 cups water
- 1 lb parboiled long grain rice
- 1/2 cup corn
- 2 tomatoes (medium, chopped)
- 1 cucumber
- 1 green pepper diced

- 1 bunch fresh parsley
- 4 fresh spearmint leaves, chopped
- 1/4 tsp Sea salt to taste
- 1/2 cup Olive oil
- Juice and zest of 1 lemon

## Instructions

1. Chop tomatoes, cucumber, pepper, parsley, and spearmint.
2. Place all vegetables with the corn and salt in your Instant Pot; stir well.
3. Add the rice over the vegetables and pour olive oil; stir.
4. Lock lid into place and set on the RICE setting for 5 minutes.
5. When the timer beeps, press "Cancel" and carefully flip the Quick Release valve to let the pressure out.
6. Carefully open the lid and transfer the rice mixtures to a serving plate.
7. <u>Prepare the dressing:</u>
8. Stir in a bowl the olive oil, lemon juice and lemon zest.
9. Combine the vegetables with rice and dressing and serve.

**Servings:** 6

**Cooking Times**

Total Time: 20 minutes

**Nutrition Facts**

Serving size: 1/6 of a recipe (12 ounces)

Percent daily values based on the Reference Daily Intake (RDI) for a 2000 calorie diet.

Nutrition information calculated from recipe ingredients.

**Amount Per Serving**

Calories 318,04

Calories From Fat (54%) 170,77

**% Daily Value**

| | |
|---|---|
| Total Fat 19,32g 30% | Total Carbohydrates 32,2g 11% |
| Saturated Fat 2,88g 14% | Fiber 2,88g 12% |
| Cholesterol 2,93mg <1% | Sugar 3,02g |
| Sodium 971,47mg 40% | Protein 4,66g 9% |
| Potassium 298,75mg 9% | |

# Mushroom Fettuccini with Sun-dried Tomato (Instant Pot)

## Ingredients

- 1/4 cup Olive oil
- 1 large onion finely chopped
- 3 cloves Garlic, minced
- 3 oz Sun Dried Tomatoes, softened and minced
- 5 oz Mushrooms mix ( Crimini, Shiitake, Oyster)
- 1 lb Fettuccini
- 3 cups water
- 1/2 cup Pine nuts

## Instructions

1. Press the "Sauté" button to heat up the insert of your Instant Pot and add the olive oil.
2. Sauté the onion and garlic with a pinch of salt.
3. Add mushrooms mix and sauté for 1 - 2 minutes.
4. Add minced Sun-dried tomatoes and stir well.
5. Place the Fettuccine over the onions and mushrooms, and pour the water.
6. Seal the lid and set it to MANUAL mode, high pressure, 8 -9 minutes cooking time.
7. Use a natural pressure release. When valve drops carefully remove the lid.
8. Serve hot and enjoy.

**Servings:** 6

**Cooking Times**

Total Time: 20 minutes

**Nutrition Facts**

Serving size: 1/6 of a recipe (9.5 ounces)

Percent daily values based on the Reference Daily Intake (RDI) for a 2000 calorie diet.

Nutrition information calculated from recipe ingredients.

**Amount Per Serving**

Calories 421,35

Calories From Fat (20%) 84,47

**% Daily Value**

Total Fat 9,95g 15%                    Saturated Fat 0,88g 4%

Cholesterol 0mg 0%

Sodium 308,06mg 13%

Potassium 740,01mg 21%

Total Carbohydrates 71,63g 24%

Fiber 4,85g 19%

Sugar 7,52g

Protein 13,89g 28%

# Penne with Collard Greens (Instant Pot)

## Ingredients

- 1/4 cup Olive oil
- 1 cup onion, chopped
- 4 cloves garlic, chopped
- 1 tsp salt
- 1 lb collard greens, chopped and rinsed
- 1 cup vegetable broth (gluten free)
- 3/4 cup water
- 1 Tbs wine vinegar
- 1 tsp hot pepper sauce
- 1 lb Penne pasta
- 1/2 cup parmesan cheese, grated

## Instructions

1. Press SAUTÉ button on your Instant Pot and heat the oil.
2. Sauté garlic and onion with a pinch of with salt.
3. Add collard greens and stir. Pour vegetable broth and water; stir.
4. Stir in vinegar and hot pepper sauce.
5. Add penne pasta on the top and stir.
6. Lock lid into place and set on the MANUAL setting for 10 minutes.
7. Use Quick Release - turn the valve from sealing to venting to release the pressure.

8. Sprinkle with parmesan cheese and serve immediately.

**Servings:** 6

**Cooking Times**

Total Time: 20 minutes

**Nutrition Facts**

Serving size: 1/6 of a recipe (10 ounces)

Percent daily values based on the Reference Daily Intake (RDI) for a 2000 calorie diet.

Nutrition information calculated from recipe ingredients.

**Amount Per Serving**

Calories 449,41

Calories From Fat (24%) 109,21

**% Daily Value**

| | |
|---|---|
| Total Fat 12,38g 19% | Total Carbohydrates 67,54g 23% |
| Saturated Fat 2,89g 14% | Fiber 6,44g 26% |
| Cholesterol 7,74mg 3% | Sugar 1,58g |
| Sodium 824,5mg 34% | Protein 15,92g 32% |
| Potassium 252,07mg 7% | |

# Perfect Cauliflower Rice with Herbs (Instant Pot)

## Ingredients

- 1 medium head of cauliflower
- 1 cup water
- 2 Tbs olive oil
- 1 tsp salt(more to taste)
- 1 tsp dried parsley
- 1 tsp cumin

- 1 tsp turmeric
- 1 tsp paprika
- 1 tsp fresh cilantro
- 1 lime wedges (or lime juice)
- 2 Tbs butter grass-fed

## Instructions

1. Wash cauliflower and trim off the leaves.
2. Put all the pieces into the steamer insert in an Instant Pot.
3. Pour one cup water under the cauliflower.
4. Lock lid into place and set on the MANUAL setting for 10 minutes.
5. After the cook timer beeps, use Quick Release - turn the valve from sealing to venting to release the pressure.
6. Remove the cauliflower to a plate and add all seasonings to taste.
7. Break up cauliflower with a potato masher.
8. Add the butter and gently stir.
9. Serve with lime slices.

**Servings:** 4

**Cooking Times**

Total Time: 20 minutes

**Nutrition Facts**

Serving size: 1/4 of a recipe (10 ounces)

Percent daily values based on the Reference Daily Intake (RDI) for a 2000 calorie diet.

Nutrition information calculated from recipe ingredients.

**Amount Per Serving**

Calories 165,58

Calories From Fat (70%) 115,83

**% Daily Value**

Total Fat 13,16g 20%

Saturated Fat 4,72g 24%

Cholesterol 15,27mg 5%

Sodium 211,79mg 9%

Potassium 646,8mg 18%

Total Carbohydrates 11,02g 4%

Fiber 4,32g 17%

Sugar 4,1g

Protein 4,18g 8%

# Red and Green Beans Stew (Instant Pot)

## Ingredients

- 3 Tbsp olive oil
- 1 onion chopped

- 2 clove garlic
- 3 leeks (white part)
- 2 medium carrot thickly sliced
- 2 pinch salt and cayenne pepper
- 1/2 cup of green beans
- 1/2 lb red beans
- 2 quarts of water

## Instructions

1. Leave a red beans to soak in water for several hours.
2. Press the "Sauté" button to heat up the insert of your Instant Pot and add the olive oil.
3. Sauté the onion, garlic, leek, and carrots for 3-4 minutes.
4. Season with salt and sauté for 2 minutes.
5. Turn off the "Sauté" button.
6. Add the red beans and the green beans and pour the water; stir well.
7. Secure the lid on the Instant Pot, turning the valve to "Sealing".
8. Select the Bean / Chili cycle and select 45 - 60 minutes.
9. After the pressure cooking time has finished using Natural Release - it takes 10 - 25 minutes to depressurize naturally.
10. When valve drops carefully remove the lid.
11. Taste and adjust salt and cayenne pepper.
12. Serve hot.

**Servings:** 8

**Cooking Times**

Total Time: 1 hour and 5 minutes\

**Nutrition Facts**

Serving size: 1/8 of a recipe (12 ounces)

Percent daily values based on the Reference Daily Intake (RDI) for a 2000 calorie diet.

Nutrition information calculated from recipe ingredients.

**Amount Per Serving**

Calories 174,88

Calories From Fat (27%) 46,85

## % Daily Value

Total Fat 5,31g 8%

Saturated Fat 0,74g 4%

Cholesterol 0mg 0%

Sodium 30,91mg 1%

Potassium 580,8mg 17%

Total Carbohydrates 25,43g 8%

Fiber 8,61g 34%

Sugar 2,97g

Protein 7,91g 16%

# Rizi-Bizi with Peas Risotto (Instant Pot)

## Ingredients

- 3 Tbs olive oil
- 2 Tbs butter
- 1 onion finely chopped
- 3 cloves garlic finely chopped
- 1 1/4 cup rice
- 2 cups of vegetable broth
- 1 1/2 cup of frozen peas
- 1 cup dry white wine
- 1/4 cup Parmesan shredded
- 5 stalks of basil finely chopped
- Salt and ground pepper to taste

## Instructions

1. Press SAUTÉ button on your Instant Pot and heat the oil and butter.
2. Sauté the onion and garlic with a pinch of salt for 3 - 4 minutes; stir.
3. Add rice, peas, broth, white wine and salt and pepper.

4. Lock lid into place and set on the RICE setting for 10 minutes.
5. Use Natural Release - it takes 10 - 25 minutes to depressurize naturally.
6. Taste and adjust seasonings.
7. Sprinkle with Parmesan and basil.
8. Serve.

**Servings:** 6

**Cooking Times**

Total Time: 40 minutes

**Nutrition Facts**

Serving size: 1/6 of a recipe (9.5 ounces)

Percent daily values based on the Reference Daily Intake (RDI) for a 2000 calorie diet.

Nutrition information calculated from recipe ingredients.

**Amount Per Serving**

Calories 385,09

Calories From Fat (30%) 115,7

**% Daily Value**

| | |
|---|---|
| Total Fat 13,22g 20% | Total Carbohydrates 50,45g 17% |
| Saturated Fat 4,37g 22% | Fiber 3,06g 12% |
| Cholesterol 13,84mg 5% | Sugar 1,4g |
| Sodium 271,25mg 11% | Protein 9,27g 19% |
| Potassium 280,04mg 8% | |

# The Simplest Pasta with Broccoli (Instant Pot)

## Ingredients

- 16 oz box Pasta (any)

- 25 oz tomato - basil sauce

- 10 oz  frozen organic Broccoli

- 4 cups water

## Instructions

1. Place Pasta, broccoli, pasta sauce and water into your Instant Pot.
2. Close and lock the lid so that the vent is sealed.
3. Lock lid into place and set on the MANUAL setting for 5 minutes.
4. Use Quick Release - turn the valve from sealing to venting to release the pressure.
5. Once pressure is released, open the lid and stir.
6. Serve warm and enjoy!

**Servings:** 6

**Cooking Times**

Total Time: 10 minutes

**Nutrition Facts**

Serving size: 1/6 of a recipe (13 ounces)

Percent daily values based on the Reference Daily Intake (RDI) for a 2000 calorie diet.

Nutrition information calculated from recipe ingredients.

**Amount Per Serving**

Calories 320,49

Calories From Fat (4%) 13,11

**% Daily Value**

Total Fat 1,45g 2%

Saturated Fat 0,21g 1%

Cholesterol 0mg 0%

Sodium 737,34mg 31%

Potassium 590,05mg 17%

Total Carbohydrates 65,04g 22%

Fiber 4,84g 19%

Sugar 5,62g

Protein 12,51g 25%

# Zesty Quinoa with Lime Coconut (Instant Pot)

## Ingredients

- 1 cup quinoa, rinsed if necessary
- 1 can (11 oz) coconut milk unsweetened
- 1/4 tsp salt and ground white pepper
- 1 small lime, zested and juiced
- 1/4 cup water

## Instructions

1. Place one cup of quinoa into a strainer and rinse thoroughly with cold water.
2. Place quinoa, canned coconut milk, water, and salt into your Instant Pot.
3. Close the lid, and press a MANUAL button and set for 10 minutes.
4. Release pressure using the Natural method, about ten minutes.
5. Open the lid: Hold the lid handle, turn the lid counterclockwise to the open position, and lift the lid up to open.
6. Do not open the lid until the pressure inside the pot is completely released.
7. Stir in the zest and juice of one small lime to taste, adjust the salt as desired.
8. Serve warm.

**Servings:** 3

**Cooking Times**

Total Time: 15 minutes

**Nutrition Facts**

Serving size: 1/3 of a recipe (7 ounces)

Percent daily values based on the Reference Daily Intake (RDI) for a 2000 calorie diet.

Nutrition information calculated from recipe ingredients.

**Amount Per Serving**

Calories 401,99

Calories From Fat (50%) 200,12

**% Daily Value**

Total Fat 23,65g 36%

Saturated Fat 18,28g 91%

Cholesterol 0mg 0%

Sodium 16,17mg <1%

Potassium 550,06mg 16%

Total Carbohydrates 41,5g 14%

Fiber 4,64g 19%

Sugar 0,38g

Protein 10,09g 20%

# S N A C K S

## "Roasted" Sweet Potato Wedges (Instant Pot)

### Ingredients

- 2 lbs sweet potatoes
- 1/4 cup olive oil
- 1 bunch fresh parsley, chopped

- 1/2 cup olive oil
- Salt and freshly ground pepper
- 2 cups of water

### Instructions

1. Wash the sweet potatoes and slice into 1/4-inch-thick wedges.
2. Place the sweet potatoes in a large mixing bowl and coat with the olive oil.
3. Sprinkle with salt and pepper and spread out on a baking sheet.
4. Pour 2 cups water into Instant Pot inner pot.
5. Place trivet in the inner pot.
6. Place a baking sheet with sweet potatoes on the trivet.
7. Lock lid into place and set on the MANUAL setting for 16 minutes.
8. Use Quick Release - turn the valve from sealing to venting to release the pressure.
9. Season salt and pepper to taste, sprinkle with parsley and serve.

**Servings:** 8

**Cooking Times**

Total Time: 25 minutes

**Nutrition Facts**

Serving size: 1/8 of a recipe (5 ounces)

Percent daily values based on the Reference Daily Intake (RDI) for a 2000 calorie diet.

Nutrition information calculated from recipe ingredients.

**Amount Per Serving**

Calories 180,31

Calories From Fat (100%) 180,15

**% Daily Value**

Total Fat 20,38g 31%

Saturated Fat 2,31g 12%

Cholesterol 0mg 0%

Sodium 0,54mg <1%

Potassium 3,05mg <1%

Total Carbohydrates 0,03g <1%

Fiber 0,02g <1%

Sugar 0g

Protein 0,02g <1%

# Baby Potatoes with Fresh Herbs (Instant Pot)

## Ingredients

- 1/4 cup extra-virgin olive oil
- 3 cloves garlic, minced
- 1/2 lb small red-skinned potatoes
- 1/2 lb small white-skinned potatoes

- 1/2 tsp fresh thyme and marjoram finely chopped
- 1/4 tsp fresh rosemary finely chopped
- 1/2 tsp fresh mint finely chopped
- Salt and freshly ground black pepper
- 2 cups of water

## Instructions

1. Place the potatoes in a large bowl.
2. In a separate bowl, whisk the herbs, garlic, and oil together until blended, and then pour over the potatoes.
3. Sprinkle generously with salt and pepper and toss to coat. Transfer the potatoes to a large baking dish.
4. Add 2 cups water to the inner stainless steel pot in the Instant Pot, and place the trivet inside.
5. Place the baking dish with potatoes on a trivet.
6. Lock lid into place and set on the MANUAL setting for 10 minutes.
7. When the timer beeps, press "Cancel" and carefully flip the Natural Release - it takes 10 - 25 minutes to depressurize naturally.
8. Serve warm.

**Servings:** 4

**Cooking Times**

Total Time: 45 minutes

**Nutrition Facts**

Serving size: 1/4 of a recipe (5 ounces)

Percent daily values based on the Reference Daily Intake (RDI) for a 2000 calorie diet.

Nutrition information calculated from recipe ingredients.

**Amount Per Serving**

Calories 221,13

Calories From Fat (55%) 120,71

**% Daily Value**

Total Fat 13,66g 21%          Saturated Fat 1,89g 9%

Cholesterol 0mg 0%

Sodium 153,74mg 6%

Potassium 628,27mg 18%

Total Carbohydrates 22,96g 8%

Fiber 2,18g 9%

Sugar 0,89g

Protein 2,52g 5%

# Catalan Breaded Eggplant (Instant Pot)

## Ingredients

- 2 Tbs ghee without additives
- 2 cloves garlic
- 2 eggplants sliced

- 2 Tbs corn flour
- Salt and pepper to taste
- 3/4 cup water

## Instructions

1. Peel the eggplants and cut into slices of about 1/2 inch.
2. Season with salt and let stay for 30 minutes.
3. Press SAUTÉ button on your Instant Pot and heat ghee.
4. Sauté garlic for 2 - 3 minutes.
5. Add the eggplant slices and sauté for 2 - 3 minutes; stir.
6. Sprinkle with the cornflour and give a good stir.
7. Pour water and stir well.
8. Lock lid into place and set on the MANUAL setting for 4 minutes.
9. When the timer beeps, press "Cancel" and carefully flip the Quick Release valve to let the pressure out.
10. Taste and adjust salt and pepper to taste.

11. Serve warm.

**Servings:** 6

**Cooking Times**

Total Time: 20 minutes

**Nutrition Facts**

Serving size: 1/6 of a recipe (8 ounces)

Percent daily values based on the Reference Daily Intake (RDI) for a 2000 calorie diet.

Nutrition information calculated from recipe ingredients.

**Amount Per Serving**

Calories 54

Calories From Fat (7%) 3,67

**% Daily Value**

Total Fat 0,44g <1%

Saturated Fat 0,08g <1%

Cholesterol 0mg 0%

Sodium 101,73mg 4%

Potassium 430,7mg 12%

Total Carbohydrates 12,55g 4%

Fiber 6,38g 26%

Sugar 4,34g

Protein 2,13g 4%

# Cheesy Kale Chips (Instant Pot)

## Ingredients

- 1 lb Kale (chopped, tough stems discarded)
- 1/4 cup garlic infused olive oil
- Salt and ground black pepper to taste
- 3/4 cup Cheddar cheese grated

## Instructions

1. Rinse and place the kale on a few sheets of kitchen paper towel to absorb the excess moisture, pat dry.
2. Clean and break kale into small pieces.
3. Pour the olive oil, and season salt and pepper to taste. Toss to coat.
4. Spread kale pieces in a single layer in a baking tray and sprinkle with grated Cheddar cheese.
5. Pour water into your Instant Pot and place the trivet.
6. Place the baking tray with kale on a trivet.
7. Lock lid into place and set on the MANUAL setting for 5 minutes.
8. When the timer beeps, press "Cancel" and carefully flip the Quick Release valve to let the pressure out.
9. Serve immediately.

**Servings:** 4

**Cooking Times**

Total Time: 20 minutes

## Nutrition Facts

Serving size: 1/4 of a recipe (5 ounces)

Percent daily values based on the Reference Daily Intake (RDI) for a 2000 calorie diet.

Nutrition information calculated from recipe ingredients.

## Amount Per Serving

Calories 142,09

Calories From Fat (48%) 68,48

## % Daily Value

Total Fat 7,82g 12%

Saturated Fat 4,57g 23%

Cholesterol 22,25mg 7%

Sodium 180,34mg 8%

Potassium 527,66mg 15%

Total Carbohydrates 11,62g 4%

Fiber 2,27g 9%

Sugar 0,11g

Protein 9,02g 18%

# Crunchy Plantain Chips (Instant Pot)

## Ingredients

- 2 Plantains
- 2 Tbsp almond butter without salt added

- 1/4 tsp sea salt
- 1 pinch paprika
- 2 cups of water

# Instructions

1. Cut plantain into slices and place in a bowl.
2. Melt the coconut butter in your microwave oven.
3. Pour the butter into the bowl with the plantain. Sprinkle with salt and paprika and toss.
4. Place plantain slices on a baking tray.
5. Pour water into your Instant Pot and place a trivet.
6. Place a tray with plantains on the trivet.
7. Lock lid into place and set on the MANUAL setting for 5 minutes.
8. When the timer beeps, press "Cancel" and carefully flip the Quick Release valve to let the pressure out.
9. Serve hot or cold.

**Servings:** 2

**Cooking Times**

Total Time: 15 minutes

**Nutrition Facts**

Serving size: 1/2 of a recipe (7.5 ounces)

Percent daily values based on the Reference Daily Intake (RDI) for a 2000 calorie diet.

Nutrition information calculated from recipe ingredients.

**Amount Per Serving**

Calories 325,31

Calories From Fat (25%) 81,95

**% Daily Value**

| | |
|---|---|
| Total Fat 9,75g 15% | Total Carbohydrates 61,43g 20% |
| Saturated Fat 0,93g 5% | Fiber 6,03g 24% |
| Sodium 2742,89mg 114% | Sugar 27,58g |
| Potassium 1018,74mg 29% | Protein 5,9g 12% |

# Cumin Sesame Pasta Cauliflower (Instant Pot)

## Ingredients

- 1/4 cup extra-virgin olive oil
- 4 cloves garlic, smashed and minced into a paste
- 2 heads cauliflower
- 4 tsp ground cumin
- salt and freshly ground black pepper
- 1/2 cup sesame paste
- 1/4 cup Lemon juice (freshly squeezed)
- 1/2 cup water

## Instructions

1. Press SAUTÉ button on your Instant Pot and heat the oil.
2. Sauté the garlic with a little salt for 2 - 3 minutes; stir.
3. Add the cauliflower, cumin, and salt and pepper and stir.
4. Lock lid into place and set on the MANUAL setting for 5 minutes.
5. When ready, use Quick Release - turn the valve from sealing to venting to release the pressure.
6. Transfer the cauliflower to a serving plate.
7. Whisk the lemon juice, sesame paste and 1/2 cup water in a small bowl and season with salt.
8. Pour the sesame paste mixture over the cauliflower and serve immediately.

**Servings:** 6

**Cooking Times**

Total Time: 40 minutes

**Nutrition Facts**

Serving size: 1/6 of a recipe (8 ounces)

Percent daily values based on the Reference Daily Intake (RDI) for a 2000 calorie diet.

Nutrition information calculated from recipe ingredients.

**Amount Per Serving**

Calories 201,08

Calories From Fat (81%) 162,73

**% Daily Value**

Total Fat 18,94g 29%

Saturated Fat 2,61g 13%

Cholesterol 0mg 0%

Sodium 18,03mg <1%

Potassium 118,62mg 3%

Total Carbohydrates 6,56g 2%

Fiber 2,04g 8%

Sugar 0,29g

Protein 3,85g 8%

# Curried Carrot Chips (Instant Pot)

## Ingredients

- 1 lb  carrots, peeled

- 1/4 cup olive oil

- 1 1/2 tsp curry powder
- 2 cups of water
- 1/4 tsp Salt and pepper (or to taste)

## Instructions

1. Wash, clean and cut carrots into thin strips.
2. Place carrot strips in large bowl.
3. Toss with olive oil, curry powder, salt, and pepper. Transfer the carrot strips to baking dish.
4. Pour water into your Instant Pot and place a trivet.
5. Place the baking dish with carrots on a trivet.
6. Lock lid into place and set on the MANUAL setting for 10 minutes.
7. When the timer beeps, press "Cancel" and carefully flip the Quick Release valve to let the pressure out.
8. Serve warm or cold.

**Servings:** 4

**Cooking Times**

Total Time: 20 minutes

**Nutrition Facts**

Serving size: 1/4 of a recipe (5 ounces)

Percent daily values based on the Reference Daily Intake (RDI) for a 2000 calorie diet.

Nutrition information calculated from recipe ingredients.

**Amount Per Serving**

Calories 170,71

Calories From Fat (72%) 123,33

**% Daily Value**

Total Fat 13,98g 22%

Saturated Fat 1,94g 10%

Cholesterol 0mg 0%

Sodium 224,86mg 9%

Potassium 386,26mg 11%

Total Carbohydrates 11,74g 4%

Fiber 3,67g 15%                    Protein 1,24g 2%

Sugar 5,42g

# Easy Beetroot Chips (Instant Pot)

## Ingredients

- 4 - 5 medium beets
- salt and black pepper (per taste)
- 1/4 cup garlic-infused olive oil
- 2 cups of water

## Instructions

1. Wash and peel beets; thinly slice a beet with a mandolin.
2. Sprinkle beetroot slices with olive oil, and salt and pepper to taste. Spray a baking dish with a cooking spray.
3. Layer beets on a baking dish.
4. Add water to the inner stainless steel pot in the Instant Pot, and place the trivet inside.
5. Place the baking dish on a trivet.
6. Lock lid into place and set on the MANUAL setting for 15 minutes.
7. Use Natural Release - it takes 10 - 25 minutes to depressurize naturally.
8. Serve warm or cold.

**Servings:** 4

**Cooking Times**

Total Time: 50 minutes

**Nutrition Facts**

Serving size: 1/4 of a recipe (4.5 ounces)

Percent daily values based on the Reference Daily Intake (RDI) for a 2000 calorie diet.

Nutrition information calculated from recipe ingredients.

**Amount Per Serving**

Calories 52,54

Calories From Fat (17%) 9,04

**% Daily Value**

Total Fat 1,03g 2%

Saturated Fat 0,15g <1%

Cholesterol 0mg 0%

Sodium 80,27mg 3%

Potassium 338,52mg 10%

Total Carbohydrates 10,05g 3%

Fiber 2,97g 12%

Sugar 6,93g

Protein 1,69g 3%

# Ginger Butternut Squash Chips (Instant Pot)

## Ingredients

- 3/4 lb butternut squash
- 2 Tbsp garlic-infused olive oil
- 1 tsp ginger
- 1/4 tsp nutmeg

- 1 tsp cinnamon
- 1/4 tsp cloves
- pinch salt

## Instructions

1. Clean and peel the butternut squash, and slice thinly on a mandolin; place the butternut squash on a shallow plate.
2. In a separate bowl, combine the oil, ginger, nutmeg, cinnamon, and cloves.
3. Pour the oil mixture over the butternut squash and toss to combine well.
4. Place the carrot slices close to each other on a baking dish lined with parchment paper.
5. Pour one cup water and place the trivet in your Instant Pot
6. Place the baking dish with carrots on the trivet.
7. Lock lid into place and set on the MANUAL setting for 10 minutes.
8. Once cooking completes let the pressure valve release naturally (about 15 minutes).
9. Serve hot.

**Servings:** 4

**Cooking Times**

Total Time: 30 minutes

**Nutrition Facts**

Serving size: 1/4 of a recipe (4 ounces)

Percent daily values based on the Reference Daily Intake (RDI) for a 2000 calorie diet.

Nutrition information calculated from recipe ingredients.

**Amount Per Serving**

Calories 100,29

Calories From Fat (61%) 61,09

**% Daily Value**

Total Fat 6,92g 11%

Saturated Fat 0,99g 5%

Cholesterol 0mg 0%

Sodium 149,32mg 6%

Potassium 304,88mg 9%

Total Carbohydrates 10,44g 3%

Fiber 1,96g 8%                    Protein 0,89g 2%

Sugar 1,93g

# Parsnip Fingers with Rosemary (Instant Pot)

## Ingredients

- 2 parsnips, sliced
- 2 Tbsp olive oil
- 1 tsp rosemary finely chopped

- Salt to taste
- 2 cups water

## Instructions

1. Wash, peel and cut the parsnip into sticks. Season salt and rosemary.
2. Pour the oil over the parsnip and toss to combine well.
3. Pour 2 cups water and trivet into Instant Pot inner pot.
4. Place the parsnip fingers on a steamer basket.
5. Lock lid into place and set on the MANUAL setting for 7 minutes.
6. When the timer beeps, press "Cancel" and carefully flip the Quick Release valve to let the pressure out.
7. Serve immediately.

**Servings:** 6

**Cooking Times**

Total Time: 15 minutes

**Nutrition Facts**

Serving size: 1/6 of a recipe (4 ounces)

Percent daily values based on the Reference Daily Intake (RDI) for a 2000 calorie diet. Nutrition information calculated from recipe ingredients.

**Amount Per Serving**

Calories 106,68

Calories From Fat (39%) 42,07

**% Daily Value**

Total Fat 4,77g 7%

Saturated Fat 0,67g 3%

Cholesterol 0mg 0%

Sodium 106,06mg 4%

Potassium 334,64mg 10%

Total Carbohydrates 16,04g 5%

Fiber 4,38g 18%

Sugar 4,27g

Protein 1,07g 2%

# SIDE DISH

## "Roasted" Jerusalem Artichokes with Parsley (Instant Pot)

### Ingredients

- 2 Tbs olive oil
- 3 cloves garlic finely chopped
- 2 lbs sunchokes (Jerusalem Artichokes)
- 1 Tbsp fresh lime juice
- 2 Tbs fresh parsley chopped
- 1/2 tsp Salt and freshly black pepper to taste

### Instructions

1. Scrub the sunchokes clean and chop into 1-inch chunks; set aside.
2. Press SAUTÉ button on your Instant Pot and heat the oil.
3. Sauté the garlic with a pinch of salt for 2 - 3 minutes: stir.
4. Add the sunchokes and lime juice and sauté for 2 minutes; stir.
5. Lock lid into place and set on the MANUAL setting for 10 minutes.
6. Use Natural Release - it takes 10 - 25 minutes to depressurize naturally.
7. Season with salt and pepper to taste.
8. Sprinkle with parsley and serve warm.

**Servings:** 6

**Cooking Times**

Total Time: 45 minutes

**Nutrition Facts**

Serving size: 1/6 of a recipe (6.5 ounces)

Percent daily values based on the Reference Daily Intake (RDI) for a 2000 calorie diet.

Nutrition information calculated from recipe ingredients.

**Amount Per Serving**

Calories 164,78

Calories From Fat (24%) 40,08

**% Daily Value**

Total Fat 4,54g 7%

Saturated Fat 0,62g 3%

Cholesterol 0mg 0%

Sodium 7,77mg <1%

Potassium 731,08mg 21%

Total Carbohydrates 29,86g 10%

Fiber 2,75g 11%

Sugar 16,07g

Protein 3,48g 7%

# Apple Mango Coleslaw (Instant Pot)

## Ingredients

- 1/3 cup garlic infused olive oil
- 2 small onions, finely sliced
- 3 cups pickled cabbage shredded
- 1 carrot, grated

- 2 medium apple, cored and chopped
- 1 small mango chopped
- 2 Tbsp brown sugar
- 1 Tbs lemon juice, or to taste
- Salt and pepper to taste

## Instructions

1. Press SAUTÉ button on your Instant Pot and heat the oil.
2. Sauté the onions with a little salt for 2 - 3 minutes.
3. Add the cabbage and sauté for 3 - 4 minutes stirring often.
4. Place all remaining ingredients and stir well.
5. Lock lid into place and set on the MANUAL setting for 12 minutes.
6. Use Quick Release - turn the valve from sealing to venting to release the pressure.
7. Taste and adjust salt and pepper to taste.
8. Serve immediately.

**Servings:** 6

**Cooking Times**

Total Time: 25 minutes

**Nutrition Facts**

Serving size: 1/6 of a recipe (7 ounces)

Percent daily values based on the Reference Daily Intake (RDI) for a 2000 calorie diet.

Nutrition information calculated from recipe ingredients.

**Amount Per Serving**

Calories 201,52

Calories From Fat (54%) 108,77

**% Daily Value**

Total Fat 12,32g 19%

Saturated Fat 1,74g 9%

Cholesterol 0mg 0%

Sodium 21,29mg <1%

Potassium 294,29mg 8%

Total Carbohydrates 23,87g 8%

Fiber 3,85g 15%

Sugar 17,79g

Protein 1,56g 3%

# Classic Vegetable Sauerkraut (Instant Pot)

## Ingredients

- 1/4 cup olive oil
- 1 medium dry onion finely chopped
- 2 carrots
- 1 1/2 lbs sauerkraut
- 1 cup vegetable broth
- 1 cup of water
- 2 bay leaves
- 1 tsp sweet paprika
- 1 Tbs fresh parsley chopped

## Instructions

1. Press SAUTÉ button on your Instant Pot and heat the olive oil.
2. Sauté onion and carrots with a little salt for 3 - 4 minutes.
3. Add the sauerkraut and sauté for 2 - 3 minutes; stir.
4. Pour the vegetable broth and water. Add the bay leaves, and season with sweet paprika, and salt and pepper.
5. Lock lid into place and set on the MANUAL setting for 12 minutes.
6. Use Quick Release - turn the valve from sealing to venting to release the pressure.
7. Add chopped parsley and stir well.
8. Taste and adjust salt and pepper to taste.
9. Serve warm.

**Servings:** 5

**Cooking Times**

Total Time: 30 minutes

**Nutrition Facts**

Serving size: 1/5 of a recipe (9 ounces)

Percent daily values based on the Reference Daily Intake (RDI) for a 2000 calorie diet.

Nutrition information calculated from recipe ingredients.

**Amount Per Serving**

Calories 146,83

Calories From Fat (67%) 98,46

**% Daily Value**

| | |
|---|---|
| Total Fat 11,15g 17% | Total Carbohydrates 11,62g 4% |
| Saturated Fat 1,57g 8% | Fiber 5,35g 21% |
| Cholesterol 0,03mg <1% | Sugar 5g |
| Sodium 945,19mg 39% | Protein 1,91g 4% |
| Potassium 380,44mg 11% | |

# Creamy Pumpkin Squash Soup (Instant Pot)

## Ingredients

- 2 Tbs garlic infused olive oil
- 1 butternut pumpkin cut in chunks
- 1 red onion finely chopped
- 1 apple, peeled, cored and grated

- 1 tsp curry powder
- 2 cups vegetable broth (gluten free)
- 2 cups water
- 3 bay leaves
- 2 cups fresh cream

## Instructions

1. Press SAUTÉ button on your Instant Pot and heat the olive oil.
2. Add the pumpkin chunks, onion, apple and a curry powder and cook for 3 - 4 minutes, Pour the vegetable broth and water; add the bay leaves.
3. Lock lid into place and set on the MANUAL setting for 7 - 8 minutes.
4. After the pressure cooking time has finished use Quick Release - turn the valve from sealing to venting to release the pressure.
5. Remove the bay leaves.
6. Pour the soup into your fast-speed blender and blend, add the cream and blend until creamy and soft.
7. Taste and adjust the seasoning to taste.
8. Serve in warmed pumpkin shells or bowls.

**Servings:** 6

**Cooking Times**

Total Time: 25 minutes

**Nutrition Facts**

Serving size: 1/6 of a recipe (11 ounces)

Percent daily values based on the Reference Daily Intake (RDI) for a 2000 calorie diet.

Nutrition information calculated from recipe ingredients.

**Amount Per Serving**

Calories 138,74

Calories From Fat (32%) 43,83

**% Daily Value**

Total Fat 4,96g 8%

Saturated Fat 2,72g 14%

Cholesterol 10,2mg 3%

Sodium 355,74mg 15%

Potassium 592,43mg 17%

Sugar 4,63g

Total Carbohydrates 21,59g 7%

Protein 4,23g 8%

Fiber 2,04g 8%

# Mushrooms and Almond Gravy (Instant Pot)

## Ingredients

- 1/4 cup butter
- 2 Tbs of extra virgin olive oil
- 3/4 lb mushrooms
- 2 cups vegetable broth
- 1 cup water
- 4 Tbs almond flour
- 1 cup almond milk
- salt and pepper to taste

## Instructions

1. Press SAUTÉ button on your Instant Pot and heat the butter and olive oil.
2. Add sliced mushroom to your Instant pot and sauté for 2 minutes.
3. Pour the broth and the water and stir well.
4. In a small bowl, whisk the almond flour with almond milk.
5. Pour the almond flour mixture over the mushrooms and stir well.
6. Lock lid into place and set on the MANUAL setting for 5 minutes.
7. When the timer beeps, press "Cancel" and carefully flip the Quick Release valve to let the pressure out.
8. Taste and adjust salt and pepper.
9. Serve hot or keep refrigerated.

**Servings:** 8

**Cooking Times**

Total Time: 15 minutes

**Nutrition Facts**

Serving size: 1/8 of a recipe (6 ounces)

Percent daily values based on the Reference Daily Intake (RDI) for a 2000 calorie diet.

Nutrition information calculated from recipe ingredients.

**Amount Per Serving**

Calories 134,69

Calories From Fat (62%) 83,75

**% Daily Value**

Total Fat 9,64g 15%

Saturated Fat 4,34g 22%

Cholesterol 16,16mg 5%

Sodium 411,6mg 17%

Potassium 271,43mg 8%

Total Carbohydrates 9,72g 3%

Fiber 1,79g 7%

Sugar 1,74g

Protein 3,91g 8%

# Pepper Squash Puree (Instant Pot)

# Ingredients

- 3 Pepper squash (acorn squash), halved, and seeded
- 3/4 tsp Kosher salt and black ground pepper
- 1/4 tsp baking soda
- 1/2 cup water
- 1/4 cup butter
- 2 Tbs sugar
- 1/2 tsp grated nutmeg

## Instructions

1. Sprinkle the cut side of the pepper squash with the salt and the baking soda.
2. Put a steaming basket in your Instant pot, pour in 1/2 cup of water, then stack the squash on top.
3. Lock lid into place and set on the MANUAL setting for 20 minutes.
4. When the timer beeps, press "Cancel" and carefully flip the Quick Release valve to let the pressure out.
5. Remove the squash from the cooker, and let cool.
6. Scrape the flesh from the squash into a medium bowl.
7. Add the butter, sugar salt and pepper, and nutmeg.
8. Mash the squash with a potato masher until the butter is melted and the squash is smooth.
9. Serve immediately.

**Servings:** 4

**Cooking Times**

Total Time: 35 minutes

**Nutrition Facts**

Serving size: 1/4 of a recipe (6 ounces)

Percent daily values based on the Reference Daily Intake (RDI) for a 2000 calorie diet.

Nutrition information calculated from recipe ingredients.

**Amount Per Serving**

Calories 186,12

Calories From Fat (55%) 102,96

**% Daily Value**

Total Fat 11,72g 18%

Saturated Fat 7,38g 37%

Cholesterol 30,5mg 10%

Sodium 86,11mg 4%

Potassium 409,29mg 12%

Total Carbohydrates 22,05g 7%

Fiber 2,35g 9%

Sugar 11,2g

Protein 1,3g 3%

# Sweet and Sour Beet Salad (Instant Pot)

## Ingredients

- 2 lbs fresh beets
- sea-salt to taste
- 1/4 cup red onion finely diced
- 1/2 cup vegetable broth
- 1/4 cup sugar (or molasses, sweetener, honey)
- 1 tsp mustard (Dijon, English, or whole grain)
- 1/4 cup Apple Cider Vinegar

## Instructions

1. Clean, peel and cut the beets into 1-inch pieces.
2. Place a steamer insert inside your Instant Pot and arrange the beets in a single layer on top.
3. Lock lid into place and set on the MANUAL setting for 15 minutes.
4. When the timer beeps, press "Cancel" and carefully flip the Quick Release valve to let the pressure out.
5. Slice the beets into 1/4 to 1/2 inch slivers.
6. Add the chopped onions and toss.

7. In a small saucepan combine the vegetable broth, salt, and pepper, sugar, mustard and vinegar. Bring to boil and remove from the heat.
8. Let cool for 5 minutes and pour the mixture over the beet slices and onions.
9. Toss to combine well and refrigerate for 4 to 6 hours.
10. Remove from refrigerator and serve at room temperature.

**Servings:** 6

**Cooking Times**

Inactive Time: 6 hours

Total Time: 30 minutes

**Nutrition Facts**

Serving size: 1/6 of a recipe (9 ounces)

Percent daily values based on the Reference Daily Intake (RDI) for a 2000 calorie diet.

Nutrition information calculated from recipe ingredients.

**Amount Per Serving**

Calories 105,15

Calories From Fat (6%) 6,02

**% Daily Value**

Total Fat 0,71g 1%

Saturated Fat 0,13g <1%

Cholesterol 0,21mg <1%

Sodium 302,89mg 13%

Potassium 695,8mg 20%

Total Carbohydrates 22,54g 8%

Fiber 6,04g 24%

Sugar 13,68g

Protein 3,85g 8%

# Sweet Potato & Pecans Casserole (Instant Pot)

## Ingredients

- 1 cup water
- 2 large sweet potatoes
- 2 Tbs butter, melted
- 1 cup sweetener of your taste
- 1 tsp vanilla
- 2 Tbs heavy cream
- 1 tsp cinnamon, ground

- 1/8 tsp nutmeg, ground
- 1 egg
- Topping
- 1 Tbs butter, melted
- 1/3 cup sugar (brown or white, as you prefer)
- 1 Tbs flour
- 1/3 cup pecans (chopped)

## Instructions

1. Peel and cut sweet potatoes in half lengthwise and cut into 1-inch slices.
2. Place a steamer basket in your Instant Pot and place sweet potatoes.
3. Lock lid into place and set on the MANUAL setting for 8 minutes.
4. Use Quick Release - turn the valve from sealing to venting to release the pressure.
5. Place sweet potatoes in a mixing bowl and add in sweetener, vanilla, butter, cinnamon, and nutmeg and beat with an electric mixer until smooth.
6. Add egg and cream, blend well. Pour into greased casserole dish.
7. Make topping: Mix up together butter, brown sugar, flour, and nuts by using a fork; scatter over the top of casserole.
8. Place in your Instant Pot. Add 1 cup water.
9. Lock lid into place and set on the MANUAL setting for 15 minutes.

10. When the timer beeps, press "Cancel" and carefully flip the Quick Release valve to let the pressure out.
11. Serve hot.

**Servings**: 6

**Cooking Times**

Total Time: 40 minutes

**Nutrition Facts**

Serving size: 1/6 of a recipe (4 ounces).

Percent daily values based on the Reference Daily Intake (RDI) for a 2000 calorie diet.

Nutrition information calculated from recipe ingredients.

**Amount Per Serving**

Calories 167,91

Calories From Fat (61%) 102,6

**% Daily Value**

Total Fat 11,86g 18%

Saturated Fat 4,87g 24%

Cholesterol 49,68mg 17%

Sodium 94,24mg 4%

Potassium 48,69mg 1%

Total Carbohydrates 13,98g 5%

Fiber 0,82g 3%

Sugar 0,9g

Protein 2,14g 4%

# Sweet Potato Puree (Instant Pot)

## Ingredients

- 3 lbs sweet potatoes, peeled
- 1 cup water
- 2 Tbs butter, unsalted
- 1 1 tsp kosher salt
- 2 tsp sugar

- 2 tsp lemon juice
- 2 pinch ground nutmeg
- 2 pinch ground cinnamon
- 1/2 cup shredded cheese (any meltable cheese: Mozzarella, Cheddar, etc)

## Instructions

1. Clean, wash and place sweet potatoes and water in your Instant Pot Cooker.
2. Lock lid into place and set on the MANUAL setting for 4 minutes.
3. When the timer beeps, press "Cancel" and carefully flip the Quick Release valve to let the pressure out.
4. Sprinkle some shredded cheese on top and put the lid back on for a couple of minutes to melt the cheese.
5. Transfer sweet potatoes to large mixing bowl.
6. Mash with potato masher or hand mixer.
7. Once thoroughly mashed, add remaining ingredients.
8. Taste and adjust seasoning to taste.
9. Serve immediately.

**Servings:** 6

**Nutrition Facts**

Serving size: 1/6 of a recipe (10 ounces)

Percent daily values based on the Reference Daily Intake (RDI) for a 2000 calorie diet.

Nutrition information calculated from recipe ingredients.

**Amount Per Serving**

Calories 71,64

Calories From Fat (69%) 49,46

**% Daily Value**

| | |
|---|---|
| Total Fat 5,63g 9% | Total Carbohydrates 2,67g <1% |
| Saturated Fat 3,57g 18% | Fiber 0,09g <1% |
| Cholesterol 17,22mg 6% | Sugar 0,3g |
| Sodium 554,14mg 23% | Protein 2,78g 6% |
| Potassium 14,22mg <1% | |

# Zucchini and Potato Puree (Instant Pot)

## Ingredients

- 2 Tbsp garlic-infused ghee
- 1 large onion
- 1 lb zucchini
- 2 medium potatoes sliced or chopped
- 1 large carrot, diced
- 1 cup vegetable broth
- 1 can (15 oz) coconut milk
- salt and pepper to taste

# Instructions

1. Clean and quarter your zucchini. Peel and chop onion and the carrot.
2. Press SAUTÉ button on your Instant Pot and heat the ghee.
3. Sauté the onion with a little salt for 2 - 3 minutes.
4. Add zucchini, potatoes, and carrots. Sauté for 3 - 4 minutes stirring occasionally.
5. Pour the broth and stir well.
6. Lock lid into place and set on the MANUAL setting for 10 minutes.
7. Use Quick Release - turn the valve from sealing to venting to release the pressure.
8. Place zucchini and potato mixture in your high-speed blender along with coconut milk.
9. Blend until smooth or until desired consistency is reached.
10. Taste and adjust salt and pepper to taste.
11. Serve immediately.

**Servings:** 6

**Cooking Times**

Total Time: 35 minutes

**Nutrition Facts**

Serving size: 1/6 of a recipe (10 ounces)

Percent daily values based on the Reference Daily Intake (RDI) for a 2000 calorie diet.

Nutrition information calculated from recipe ingredients.

**Amount Per Serving**

Calories 240,44

Calories From Fat (56%) 135,21

**% Daily Value**

Total Fat 16,11g 25%

Saturated Fat 13,65g 68%

Sodium 348,51mg 15%

Potassium 748,72mg 21%

Total Carbohydrates 22,64g 8%

Fiber 3,36g 13%

Sugar 3,87g

Protein 4,93g 10%

# PASTA

## "Baked" Fusilli with Spinach and Lemon (Instant Pot)

## Ingredients

- 1/4 cup olive oil
- 2 cups onion finely chopped
- 4 cloves garlic minced
- 1/2 lb fresh baby spinach
- 3/4 lb Fusilli pasta
- 1/2 cup dry white wine
- 1/2 tsp salt and ground black pepper to taste
- 1/4 tsp grated lemon rind
- 1 cup Parmigiano-Reggiano grated
- Water (to cover completely pasta)

## Instructions

1. Press SAUTÉ button on your Instant Pot and heat the oil.
2. Sauté the onion and garlic with a little salt for 3 - 4 minutes or until soft.
3. Add all remaining ingredients and stir well.
4. Lock lid into place and set on the MANUAL setting for 5 minutes.
5. When the timer beeps, press "Cancel" and carefully flip the Quick Release valve to let the pressure out.
6. Transfer pasta mixture to a serving plate.
7. Sprinkle some more cheese and some lemon juice and rind.
8. Serve.

**Servings:** 6

**Cooking Times**

Total Time: 1 hour and 35 minutes

**Nutrition Facts**

Serving size: 1/6 of a recipe (8.5 ounces)

Percent daily values based on the Reference Daily Intake (RDI) for a 2000 calorie diet.

Nutrition information calculated from recipe ingredients.

**Amount Per Serving**

Calories 376,51

Calories From Fat (24%) 90,98

**% Daily Value**

Total Fat 10,26g 16%

Saturated Fat 1,44g 7%

Cholesterol 0mg 0%

Sodium 38,5mg 2%

Potassium 421,42mg 12%

Total Carbohydrates 57,44g 19%

Fiber 3,43g 14%

Sugar 2,63g

Protein 10,34g 21%

# Appetizing Balsamic Pasta Salad (Instant Pot)

# Ingredients

- 1/4 cup extra-virgin olive oil
- 1 onion sliced
- 2 Tbsp garlic minced
- 1/2 cup corn boiled
- 1 carrot chopped
- 6 olives without kernel
- 2 dried tomatoes
- 1/2 lb of pasta (any)
- 1 tsp honey
- 1 tsp mustard
- 1 Tbs balsamic vinegar
- Salt to taste

## Instructions

1. Press SAUTÉ button on your Instant Pot and heat the oil.
2. Sauté the onion with a pinch of salt for 3 - 4 minutes.
3. Add carrot, olives, corn, and tomatoes and sauté for 2 minutes.
4. Add pasta and remaining ingredients and pour the water.
5. Season salt and pepper to taste and stir well.
6. Lock lid into place and set on the MANUAL setting for 4 minutes.
7. Use Quick Release - turn the valve from sealing to venting to release the pressure.
8. Taste and adjust salt and pepper.
9. Serve warm.

**Servings:** 2

**Cooking Times**

Total Time: 30 minutes

**Nutrition Facts**

Serving size: 1/2 of a recipe (9.5 ounces)

Percent daily values based on the Reference Daily Intake (RDI) for a 2000 calorie diet.

Nutrition information calculated from recipe ingredients.

**Amount Per Serving**

Calories 394,2

Calories From Fat (69%) 272,1

**% Daily Value**

Total Fat 30,94g 48%

Saturated Fat 4,28g 21%

Cholesterol 0mg 0%

Sodium 594,42mg 25%

Potassium 397,34mg 11%

Total Carbohydrates 29,57g 10%

Fiber 4,67g 19%

Sugar 10,54g

Protein 3,55g 7%

# Cold Pasta with Potatoes and Pesto (Instant Pot)

## Ingredients

- 1/2 lb of pasta (any)
- 2 medium potatoes sliced or chopped
- 2 Tbs extra virgin olive oil
- 1/4 tsp salt or to taste
- 2 cups water
- 1/2 cup pesto sauce

## Instructions

1. Place pasta, potatoes, olive oil and salt to Instant Pot's inner pot/liner.
2. Pour the water and stir.
3. Lock lid into place and set on the MANUAL setting for 10 minutes.
4. Use Natural Release - it takes 10 - 25 minutes to depressurize naturally.
5. Transfer pasta and potato to a serving bowl and combine with pesto sauce.
6. Taste and adjust salt to taste.
7. Refrigerate for 2 hours.
8. Serve.

**Servings:** 3

**Cooking Times**

Total Time: 35 minutes

**Nutrition Facts**

Serving size: 1/3 of a recipe (9 ounces)

Percent daily values based on the Reference Daily Intake (RDI) for a 2000 calorie diet.

Nutrition information calculated from recipe ingredients.

**Amount Per Serving**

Calories 589,35

Calories From Fat (34%) 201,59

**% Daily Value**

Total Fat 22,84g 35%

Saturated Fat 4,59g 23%

Cholesterol 7,68mg 3%

Sodium 390,25mg 16%

Potassium 728,78mg 21%

Total Carbohydrates 59,83g 22%

Fiber 4,91g 20%

Sugar 0,96g

Protein 16,52g 33%

# Double Cheese and Jalapeno Rigatoni (Instant Pot)

## Ingredients

- 2 Tbs butter, divided
- 2 Tbsp garlic infused olive oil
- 1/2 cup green onions sliced
- 1 cup red bell pepper
- 1 Tbs jalapeno pepper
- 5 cups uncooked rigatoni
- 1 cup Fontina cheese shredded
- 1 cup Cheddar cheese shredded
- 3/4 tsp salt
- Water for cooking

## Instructions

1. Press SAUTÉ button on your Instant Pot and heat the butter and the oil.
2. Sauté the onion with a pinch of salt for 3 - 4 minutes or until soft.
3. Add red pepper and Jalapeno pepper and sauté for 2 minutes, stirring occasionally.
4. Add rigatoni pasta and water; stir.
5. At the end, add the cheeses.
6. Lock lid into place and set on the MANUAL setting for 4 minutes.
7. When the timer beeps, press "Cancel" and carefully flip the Quick Release valve to let the pressure out.
8. Serve warm.

**Servings:** 6

**Cooking Times**

Total Time: 40 minutes

**Nutrition Facts**

Serving size: 1/6 of a recipe (10 ounces)

Percent daily values based on the Reference Daily Intake (RDI) for a 2000 calorie diet.

Nutrition information calculated from recipe ingredients.

**Amount Per Serving**

Calories 383,91

Calories From Fat (53%) 203,1

**% Daily Value**

Total Fat 22,85g 35%                    Saturated Fat 13,14g 66%

Cholesterol 71,81mg 24%

Sodium 1254,8mg 52%

Potassium 105,59mg 3%

Total Carbohydrates 24,16g 8%

Fiber 3,09g 12%

Sugar 8,03g

Protein 20,06g 40%

## Farfalle with Peas, Corn and Tartar Sauce (Instant Pot)

### Ingredients

- 1/4 cup olive oil
- 1 onion, finely chopped
- 1 cup peas
- 1 can corn
- 3 sweet colored peppers, finely chopped

- 1 Tbs fennel, finely chopped
- 1 lb Farfalle pasta
- 2 Tbs of tartar sauce
- Salt and ground pepper to taste
- 3 cups water

### Instructions

1. Press SAUTÉ button on your Instant Pot and heat the oil.
2. Sauté the onion for 3 - 4 minutes until soft.
3. Add peas, corn, and peppers with a pinch of salt and pepper.
4. Sauté the vegetables for 2 minutes; stir.
5. Add all remaining ingredients and stir (make sure that the water covers the pasta).
6. Lock lid into place and set on the MANUAL setting for 5 minutes.
7. Use Quick Release - turn the valve from sealing to venting to release the pressure.
8. Taste and adjust salt and pepper.
9. Add some more tartar sauce and serve immediately.

**Servings:** 6

**Cooking Times**

Total Time: 15 minutes

**Nutrition Facts**

Serving size: 1/6 of a recipe (9.5 ounces)

Percent daily values based on the Reference Daily Intake (RDI) for a 2000 calorie diet.

Nutrition information calculated from recipe ingredients.

**Amount Per Serving**

Calories 499,27

Calories From Fat (19%) 97,04

**% Daily Value**

Total Fat 10,97g 17%

Saturated Fat 1,49g 7%

Cholesterol 0mg 0%

Sodium 171,96mg 7%

Potassium 1180,01mg 34%

Total Carbohydrates 52,66g 22%

Fiber 12,8g 51%

Sugar 7,26g

Protein 18,28g 37%

# Lemon-Mint Pasta with Peas and Artichokes (Instant Pot)

## Ingredients

- 1/4 olive oil

- 3 fresh onions, finely chopped

- 3/4 lb short pasta (any)

- 1/2 lb fresh peas

- 3 artichokes prepared

- 1 fennel, finely chopped

- 2 fresh lemon juice

- 3 Tbs mint, finely chopped

- Salt and black ground pepper

- Water

## Instructions

1. Pour the oil into your Instant Pot's inner pot/liner.
2. Add all remaining ingredients and water (to cover pasta); stir well.
3. Lock lid into place and set on the MANUAL setting for 5 minutes.
4. After the pressure cooking time has finished use Quick Release - turn the valve from sealing to venting to release the pressure.
5. Once all of the pressure releases the steam will no longer come out of the vent and you'll be able to open the lid.
6. Place the pasta mixture in a shallow serving plate with lemon slices.

**Servings:** 8

**Cooking Times**

Total Time: 15 minutes

**Nutrition Facts**

Serving size: 1/8 of a recipe (10.5 ounces)

Percent daily values based on the Reference Daily Intake (RDI) for a 2000 calorie diet.

Nutrition information calculated from recipe ingredients.

**Amount Per Serving**

Calories 388,52

Calories From Fat (11%) 42,17

**% Daily Value**

Total Fat 4,81g 7%

Saturated Fat 0,64g 3%

Cholesterol 0mg 0%

Sodium 161,78mg 7%

Potassium 1009,47mg 29%

Total Carbohydrates 52,47g 20%

Fiber 18,01g 72%

Sugar 4,58g

Protein 18,64g 37%

# Pasta Salad with Vegetables and Yogurt Dressing (Instant Pot)

## Ingredients

### Pasta

- 2 Tbs Olive oil
- 2 fresh onions, cut into thin slices
- 1/4 cup chopped onion
- 2 cups of fresh spinach finely chopped
- 1 large cucumber, sliced
- 1 cup tomato finely chopped

- 3 cups of raw pasta (whatever you prefer)

**Water**

- For yogurt dressing
- 1/2 cup Greek yogurt, drained
- 1/2 cup of cream
- 1/2 cup olive oil
- 3 Tbs of balsamic vinegar
- 2 tsp of dill
- Salt and freshly ground pepper to taste

# Instructions

1. Place all ingredients for the pasta in Instant Pot's inner pot/liner.
2. Pour water to cover completely pasta and stir well.
3. Lock lid into place and set on the MANUAL setting for 4 minutes.
4. When the timer beeps, press "Cancel" and carefully flip the Quick Release valve to let the pressure out.
5. Remove pasta mixture to the shallow bowl and let cool.
6. Combine all ingredients for the yogurt dressing and pour over pasta.
7. Before serving, put it in the refrigerator for a while and your pasta is ready!
8. Serve.

**Servings:** 6

**Cooking Times**

Total Time: 15 minutes

**Nutrition Facts**

Serving size: 1/6 of a recipe (11 ounces)

Percent daily values based on the Reference Daily Intake (RDI) for a 2000 calorie diet.

Nutrition information calculated from recipe ingredients.

**Amount Per Serving**

Calories 519,82

Calories From Fat (51%) 265,75

**% Daily Value**

Total Fat 30,1g 46%

Saturated Fat 7,72g 39%

Cholesterol 27,17mg 9%

Sodium 123,92mg 5%

Potassium 382,36mg 11%

Total Carbohydrates 52,56g 18%

Fiber 4,04g 16%

Sugar 6,12g

Protein 9,16g 18%

# Pasta with Black Olives and Pine Nuts

## Ingredients

- 1/2 lb of short pasta (fusilli, penne, celery ..)
- 2 oz of fresh arugula
- 2 Tbs of pine nuts
- 2 Tbs Parmesan grated
- 6 fresh tomatoes chopped
- 12 pitted black olives
- 2 Tbs olive oil
- 2 pinch of salt
- Water for cooking

## Instructions

1. Place all ingredients in your Instant Pot's inner pot/liner; stir.
2. Lock lid into place and set on the MANUAL setting for 5 minutes.
3. When the timer beeps, press "Cancel" and carefully flip the Quick Release valve to let the pressure out.
4. Taste and adjust seasonings.
5. Serve immediately.

**Servings:** 4

**Cooking Times**

Total Time: 10 minutes

**Nutrition Facts**

Serving size: 1/4 of a recipe (12 ounces)

Percent daily values based on the Reference Daily Intake (RDI) for a 2000 calorie diet.

Nutrition information calculated from recipe ingredients.

**Amount Per Serving**

Calories 391,77

Calories From Fat (33%) 130,31

**% Daily Value**

Total Fat 14,82g 23%

Saturated Fat 1,77g 9%

Cholesterol 2,2mg <1%

Sodium 382,44mg 16%

Potassium 659,36mg 19%

Total Carbohydrates 54,59g 18%

Fiber 4,25g 17%

Sugar 5,8g

Protein 11,36g 23%

# Pasta with Colorful Peppers and Tomato (Instant Pot)

## Ingredients

- 1/4 cup extra-virgin olive oil
- 1 cup yellow onion finely chopped
- 2 clove of garlic
- 3 medium peppers (yellow, red, green)
- 4-5 tomatoes chopped
- 1/2 lb  pasta (any)
- 1 Tbs fresh basil finely chopped
- 1/4 tsp salt and pepper

## Instructions

1. Press SAUTÉ button on your Instant Pot and heat the oil.
2. Sauté the onion and garlic until soft, for about 3 - 4  minutes.
3. Add the peppers and pinch of salt and sauté for 2 - 3 minutes.
4. Add tomatoes and sauté all together for 2 minutes; stir.
5. Add pasta and fresh basil and pour the water enough to cover pasta; stir well.
6. Lock lid into place and set on the MANUAL setting for 4 minutes.
7. When the timer beeps, press "Cancel" and carefully flip the Quick Release valve to let the pressure out.
8. Taste and adjust salt and pepper to taste.
9. Serve immediately or refrigerate for 2 hours.

**Servings:** 4

**Cooking Times**

Total Time: 20 minutes

**Nutrition Facts**

Serving size: 1/4 of a recipe (12 ounces).

Percent daily values based on the Reference Daily Intake (RDI) for a 2000 calorie diet.

Nutrition information calculated from recipe ingredients.

**Amount Per Serving**

Calories 421,39

Calories From Fat (37%) 154,32

**% Daily Value**

Total Fat 17,39g 27%

Saturated Fat 2,4g 12%

Cholesterol 0mg 0%

Sodium 19,66mg <1%

Potassium 706,84mg 20%

Total Carbohydrates 56,92g 19%

Fiber 6,1g 24%

Sugar 8,17g

Protein 10,07g 20%

# Penne with Zucchini and Pesto (Instant Pot)

## Ingredients

- 2 Tbs olive oil
- 2 cloves of garlic
- 1/2 tsp fine salt
- 2 medium zucchini
- 5 tomatoes finely chopped

- 1/4 cup of pesto
- 1/2 cup of mozzarella shredded
- 1 Tbs Italian herb mix
- 1/2 lb of short pasta (penne, penne, farfalle ..)
- Water for cooking

## Instructions

1. Press SAUTÉ button on your Instant Pot and heat the oil.
2. Sauté the garlic for 2 minutes with a pinch of salt (do not burn).
3. Add the zucchini and tomatoes and sauté for 2 - 3 minutes stirring occasionally.
4. Add pasta and all remaining ingredients; stir well.
5. Lock lid into place and set on the MANUAL setting for 5 minutes.
6. When the timer beeps, press "Cancel" and carefully flip the Quick Release valve to let the pressure out.
7. Serve hot.

**Servings:** 4

**Cooking Times**

Total Time: 15 minutes

**Nutrition Facts**

Serving size: 1/4 of a recipe (12 ounces)

Percent daily values based on the Reference Daily Intake (RDI) for a 2000 calorie diet.

Nutrition information calculated from recipe ingredients.

**Amount Per Serving**

Calories 396,17

Calories From Fat (33%) 129,26

**% Daily Value**

Total Fat 14,7g 23%

Saturated Fat 3,9g 20%

Cholesterol 13,44mg 4%

Sodium 477,77mg 20%

Potassium 579,69mg 17%

Total Carbohydrates 51,11g 17%

Fiber 4,68g 19%

Sugar 5,62g

Protein 15,1g 30%

# S A U C E S/D I P

## Aromatic Marinara Sauce (Instant Pot)

### Ingredients

- 2 can (11 oz) crushed tomatoes
- 1 can (11 oz) tomato paste, without salt, added
- 1 Tbs dried basil
- 1 Tbs dried oregano
- 1 Tbs balsamic vinegar
- 1 Tbs brown sugar
- 1 yellow onion finely chopped
- 1 Tbs minced garlic
- 2 pinches Salt and black pepper to taste

### Instructions

1. Cut the onion into a small dice and mince the garlic.
2. Place all ingredients in your Instant Pot's inner pot/liner.
3. Lock lid into place and set on the MANUAL setting for 10 minutes.
4. When the timer beeps, press "Cancel" and carefully flip the Quick Release valve to let the pressure out.
5. Taste and adjust salt and pepper.
6. Keep refrigerated up to one week.

**Servings:** 10

**Cooking Times**

Total Time: 20 minutes

**Nutrition Facts**

Serving size: 1/10 of a recipe (4.5 ounces)

Percent daily values based on the Reference Daily Intake (RDI) for a 2000 calorie diet.

Nutrition information calculated from recipe ingredients.

**Amount Per Serving**

Calories 50,69

Calories From Fat (20%) 10,35

**% Daily Value**

Total Fat 1,17g 2%

Saturated Fat 0,18g <1%

Cholesterol 0mg 0%

Sodium 266,4mg 11%

Potassium 377,01mg 11%

Total Carbohydrates 9,87g 3%

Fiber 2,04g 8%

Sugar 5,83g

Protein 1,72g 3%

# Cheesemania Dip (Instant Pot)

## Ingredients

- 1 cup water
- 3/4 lb Asiago cheese slices
- 1 cup cream cheese
- 1 cup Cheddar shredded

- 1 can (6 oz) smoked tomatoes
- 1 Tbs butter
- 1 Tbs garlic minced
- 1 tsp oregano

## Instructions

1. Put one cup of water in the bottom of your Instant Pot.
2. Cover the bottom of an Instant Pot safe bowl with tin foil and place on a trivet that has been placed on the bottom of your Instant Pot.
3. Place all ingredients on the list and cover top of the bowl with tin foil.
4. Lock lid into place and set on the MANUAL setting for 18 minutes.
5. When the timer beeps, press "Cancel" and carefully flip the Quick Release valve to let the pressure out.
6. Remove tin foil and whisk immediately until smooth.
7. Serve warm or keep refrigerated.

**Servings:** 10

**Cooking Times**

Total Time: 25 minutes

**Nutrition Facts**

Serving size: 1/10 of a recipe (4 ounces)

Percent daily values based on the Reference Daily Intake (RDI) for a 2000 calorie diet.

Nutrition information calculated from recipe ingredients.

**Amount Per Serving**

Calories 262,63

Calories From Fat (76%) 199,8

**% Daily Value**

Total Fat 22,59g 35%

Saturated Fat 13,67g 68%

Cholesterol 70,81mg 24%

Sodium 585,58mg 24%

Potassium 81,75mg 2%

Total Carbohydrates 2,83g <1%

Fiber 0,26g 1%

Sugar 1,23g

Protein 12,92g 26%

# Cherry - Raspberry Sauce (Instant Pot)

## Ingredients

- 1 cup frozen unsweetened tart cherries, thawed and well drained
- 1/2 cup fresh raspberry
- 2 Tbsp tapioca starch
- 1/2 cup honey
- 1/3 cup cherry juice blend
- 1/2 cup almonds finely chopped or ground

- 1 tsp grated orange peel

## Instructions

1. Place all ingredients in Instant Pot's inner pot/liner; stir well.
2. Lock lid into place and set on the MANUAL setting for 4 minutes.
3. Use Natural Release - it takes 10 - 25 minutes to depressurize naturally.
4. Stir well and place in a glass jar.
5. Serve immediately or keep refrigerated.

**Servings:** 8

**Cooking Times**

Total Time: 35 minutes

**Nutrition Facts**

Serving size: 1/8 of a recipe (3 ounces)

Percent daily values based on the Reference Daily Intake (RDI) for a 2000 calorie diet.

Nutrition information calculated from recipe ingredients.

**Amount Per Serving**

Calories 169,56

Calories From Fat (24%) 41,04

**% Daily Value**

Total Fat 4,91g 8%

Saturated Fat 0,47g 2%

Cholesterol 0mg 0%

Sodium 11,41mg <1%

Potassium 114mg 3%

Total Carbohydrates 32,45g 11%

Fiber 1,06g 4%

Sugar 14,87g

Protein 1,46g 3%

# Creamy Artichoke and Spinach Dip (Instant Pot)

## Ingredients

- 1/4 cup  butter unsalted, preferably grass-fed
- 1  onion, diced
- 2 Tbsp minced garlic
- 1 tsp Salt and ground black pepper
- 1 can (11 oz) artichoke hearts, chopped
- 2 cups of frozen spinach
- 1 cup  mayonnaise
- 1 tsp red pepper flakes (more or less to taste)
- 1 can (6 oz) green chili, drained
- 1 Tbsp wine vinegar
- 1/2 cup cream cheese

## Instructions

1. Press SAUTÉ button on your Instant Pot and heat the butter.
2. Sauté the onion and garlic with a pinch of salt for 3 - 4 minutes.
3. Add the artichokes and spinach and sauté for 2 - 3 minutes.
4. Add all remaining ingredients, season salt, and pepper and give a good stir.
5. Lock lid into place and set on the MANUAL setting for 15 minutes.
6. After the pressure cooking time has finished use Natural Release - it takes 10 - 25 minutes to depressurize naturally.
7. Give a good stir and serve.
8. Keep refrigerated.

**Servings:** 12

## Cooking Times

Total Time: 50 minutes

## Nutrition Facts

Serving size: 1/12 of a recipe (3.5 ounces)

Percent daily values based on the Reference Daily Intake (RDI) for a 2000 calorie diet.

Nutrition information calculated from recipe ingredients.

## Amount Per Serving

Calories 171,46

Calories From Fat (71%) 121,69

## % Daily Value

Total Fat 13,82g 21%

Saturated Fat 5,27g 26%

Cholesterol 25,89mg 9%

Sodium 246,76mg 10%

Potassium 204,73mg 6%

Total Carbohydrates 11,26g 4%

Fiber 2,42g 10%

Sugar 2,04g

Protein 2,47g 5%

# Fresh Mushroom Sauce (Instant Pot)

## Ingredients

- 2 Tbsp olive oil
- 3/4 lb fresh white mushrooms, sliced
- 2 cups plum tomatoes, chopped
- 1/2 cup scallions, sliced

- 2 tsp minced garlic
- 1/2 cup stone-ground mustard
- 1/2 tsp Salt and black pepper to taste

## Instructions

1. Place all ingredients (except mustard) to your Instant Pot.
2. Lock lid into place and set on the MANUAL setting for 5 minutes.
3. When the timer beeps, press "Cancel" and carefully flip the Quick Release valve to let the pressure out.
4. Carefully open the lid.
5. Add the mustard and stir well.
6. Serve or keep refrigerated.

**Servings:** 6

**Cooking Times**

Total Time: 10 minutes

**Nutrition Facts**

Serving size: 1/6 of a recipe (5.5 ounces)

Percent daily values based on the Reference Daily Intake (RDI) for a 2000 calorie diet.

Nutrition information calculated from recipe ingredients.

**Amount Per Serving**

Calories 86,11

Calories From Fat (62%) 53,13

**% Daily Value**

Total Fat 6,48g 10%

Saturated Fat 0,67g 3%

Cholesterol 0mg 0%

Sodium 473,5mg 20%

Potassium 376,42mg 11%

Total Carbohydrates 6,52g 2%

Fiber 1,7g 7%

Sugar 2,9g

Protein 4,03g 8%

# Honey Quince and Apple Sauce (Instant Pot)

## Ingredients

- 3 medium quinces, peeled, quartered, and cored
- 4 apples, peeled, chopped without pits
- 1/2 cup organic honey
- 1 cinnamon stick
- 1/2 vanilla bean, split
- 1/2 star anise
- 1 Tbsp lemon juice (and zest of, finely grated)

## Instructions

1. Place all ingredients from the list to Instant Pot's inner pot/liner.
2. Lock lid into place and set on the MANUAL setting for 10 minutes.
3. Naturally, release pressure for 5 minutes and quick release remaining pressure.
4. Remove cinnamon stick and star anise.
5. Let it cool and store in a glass jar.
6. Keep refrigerated.

**Servings:** 6

**Cooking Times**

Total Time: 20 minutes

**Nutrition Facts**

Serving size: 1/6 of a recipe (6.5 ounces)

Percent daily values based on the Reference Daily Intake (RDI) for a 2000 calorie diet. Nutrition information calculated from recipe ingredients.

**Amount Per Serving**

Calories 210,93

Calories From Fat (1%) 3,14

**% Daily Value**

| | |
|---|---|
| Total Fat 0,38g <1% | Total Carbohydrates 55,19g 18% |
| Saturated Fat 0,06g <1% | Fiber 5,73g 23% |
| Cholesterol 0mg 0% | Sugar 23,21g |
| Sodium 12,34mg <1% | Protein 2,45g 5% |
| Potassium 365,09mg 10% | |

# Mandarin Peach Sauce (Instant Pot)

## Ingredients

- 3 cups sliced peaches
- 4 Tbs tamari sauce
- 2 Tbs rice flour
- 1/4 tsp fennel
- 1/4 tsp black pepper
- 1/8 tsp ground cloves
- 1/8 tsp garlic powder

# Instructions

1. Place all ingredients in your Instant Pot; stir well.
2. Lock lid into place and set on the MANUAL setting for 10 minutes.
3. Use Natural Release - it takes 10 - 25 minutes to depressurize naturally. Transfer the peach mixture to your blender and blend until completely smooth and creamy.
4. Store in a glass jar and keep refrigerated.

**Servings:** 6

**Cooking Times**

Total Time: 20 minutes

**Nutrition Facts**

Serving size: 1/6 of a recipe (4 ounces)

Percent daily values based on the Reference Daily Intake (RDI) for a 2000 calorie diet.

Nutrition information calculated from recipe ingredients.

**Amount Per Serving**

Calories 53,16

Calories From Fat (5%) 2,83

**% Daily Value**

| | |
|---|---|
| Total Fat 0,34g <1% | Total Carbohydrates 11,47g 4% |
| Saturated Fat 0,04g <1% | Fiber 1,6g 6% |
| Cholesterol 0mg 0% | Sugar 7,37g |
| Sodium 670,82mg 28% | Protein 2,31g 5% |
| Potassium 200,28mg 6% | |

# Marinated Artichoke Dip (Instant Pot)

## Ingredients

- 2 can (15 oz) marinated artichoke hearts
- 2 Tbsp diced green chiles, drained
- 1/2 cup mayonnaise
- 1 cup Greek yogurt

## Instructions

1. Drain artichokes, reserving marinade; chop artichokes coarsely.
2. Place all ingredients in Instant Pot's inner pot/liner.
3. Lock lid into place and set on the MANUAL setting for 10 minutes.
4. Use Quick Release - turn the valve from sealing to venting to release the pressure.
5. Stir gently to mix ingredients, then blend in 1/2 to 1 tablespoon of the reserved artichoke marinade to give the mixture a good dipping consistency.
6. Serve hot.

**Servings:** 8

**Cooking Times**

Total Time: 15 minutes

**Nutrition Facts**

Serving size: 1/8 of a recipe (6 ounces)

Percent daily values based on the Reference Daily Intake (RDI) for a 2000 calorie diet.

Nutrition information calculated from recipe ingredients.

**Amount Per Serving**

Calories 110,88

Calories From Fat (40%) 44,58

**% Daily Value**

Total Fat 5,07g 8%

Saturated Fat 0,72g 4%

Cholesterol 3,82mg 1%

Sodium 230,35mg 10%

Potassium 381,64mg 11%

Total Carbohydrates 15,5g 5%

Fiber 5,76g 23%

Sugar 1,01g

Protein 3,85g 8%

# Moroccan Pearl Onion Sauce (Instant Pot)

## Ingredients

- 1/4 cup butter unsalted, preferably grass-fed
- 1/2 lb Pearl onions (fresh)
- 3 Tbs balsamic vinegar
- 1 cup white wine

- 2 whole cloves
- 1/2 tsp fresh lemon peels, grated
- 1 1/2 dates, chopped
- 1 1/2 cups cranberries, whole
- 1/4 cup orange juice

## Instructions

1. Trim ends from onions; rinse with cold water and remove skins.
2. Press SAUTÉ button on your Instant Pot and melt the butter.
3. Sauté the pearl onions for 3 - 4 minutes, Stir in vinegar, wine, cloves and lemon peel; stir.
4. Lock lid into place and set on the MANUAL setting for 20 minutes.
5. Naturally, release pressure for 5 minutes and quick release remaining pressure.
6. Stir in dates and cranberries; Press SAUTÉ button on your Instant Pot and saute the mixture for about 2 - 3 minutes stirring occasionally.
7. At the end, add the orange juice and stir well. Remove cloves.
8. Let cool at room temperature and store in a glass jar.
9. Keep refrigerated.

**Servings:** 6

**Cooking Times**

Total Time: 35 minutes

**Nutrition Facts**

Serving size: 1/6 of a recipe (5 ounces)

Percent daily values based on the Reference Daily Intake (RDI) for a 2000 calorie diet.

Nutrition information calculated from recipe ingredients.

**Amount Per Serving**

Calories 146,21

Calories From Fat (47%) 68,61

**% Daily Value**

Total Fat 7,82g 12%

Saturated Fat 4,89g 24%

Cholesterol 20,34mg 7%

Sodium 7,63mg <1%

Potassium 154,83mg 4%

Total Carbohydrates 12,08g 4%

Fiber 2,19g 9%

Sugar 6,48g

Protein 0,81g 2%

# Roasted Red Peppers and Basil-Nuts Dressing (Instant Pot)

## Ingredients

- 1/4 cup Olive oil
- 3 cups roasted red peppers finely chopped
- 4 clove garlic, minced
- 3/4 cup fresh basil (chopped)
- 1/4 cup nuts, minced
- 2 Tbsp red wine vinegar
- 1 tsp dried oregano
- salt and pepper to taste

## Instructions

1. Place all ingredients from the list to Instant Pot's inner pot/liner.
2. Lock lid into place and set on the MANUAL setting for 10 minutes.
3. Use Natural Release - it takes 10 - 25 minutes to depressurize naturally.
4. Let cool and store in a glass jar.
5. Serve cold with your favorite vegetables or bread.

**Servings**: 6

**Cooking Times**

Total Time: 40 minutes

**Nutrition Facts**

Serving size: 1/6 of a recipe (5 ounces)

Percent daily values based on the Reference Daily Intake (RDI) for a 2000 calorie diet.

Nutrition information calculated from recipe ingredients.

**Amount Per Serving**

Calories 231,89

Calories From Fat (72%) 168,08

**% Daily Value**

Total Fat 19,59g 30%

Saturated Fat 2,01g 10%

Cholesterol 0mg 0%

Sodium 149,37mg 6%

Potassium 415,72mg 12%

Total Carbohydrates 12,93g 4%

Fiber 5,72g 23%

Sugar 0,85g

Protein 4,95g 10%

# <u>S W E E T S</u>

## 4 Ingredients Cornbread Cake (Instant Pot)

### Ingredients

- 18.5 oz cornbread mix
- 1 large egg
- 1/2 cup oil
- 3/4 cup milk
- 1 cup water

### Instructions

1. Beat cornbread mix, egg, oil and milk just until moistened.
2. Pour the batter into the greased cake pan.
3. Cover the cake pan with paper towel and then aluminum foil.
4. Pour water into your Instant Pot and place the trivet with the cake pan.
5. Lock lid in a place, press the "CAKE" button and set the mode to "Normal".
6. Adjust the cook time to 45 minutes.
7. After the pressure cooking time has finished Use Natural Release - it takes 10 - 25 minutes to depressurize naturally.
8. Let cool for 10 minutes, slice and serve.

**Servings:** 8

**Cooking Times**

Total Time: 1 hour and 20 minutes

**Nutrition Facts**

Serving size: 1/8 of a recipe (5 ounces)

Percent daily values based on the Reference Daily Intake (RDI) for a 2000 calorie diet.

Nutrition information calculated from recipe ingredients.

**Amount Per Serving**

Calories 413,75

Calories From Fat (48%) 198,98

**% Daily Value**

Total Fat 22,55g 35%

Saturated Fat 4,37g 22%

Cholesterol 26,39mg 9%

Sodium 556,41mg 23%

Potassium 115,16mg 3%

Total Carbohydrates 46,71g 16%

Fiber 4,26g 17%

Sugar 14,52g

Protein 6,13g 12%

# Choco - Maraschino Cherries Cake (Instant Pot)

## Ingredients

- 18 oz package food cake mix
- 3/4 cup green maraschino cherries
- 1 cup red maraschino cherries
- 1/2 cup candied pineapple chunks, chopped
- 1 cup sour cream
- 3 eggs
- 1 1/2 cups nut mix (walnuts, hazelnuts, almonds...etc.) finely chopped
- 1 cup dark chocolate chips (73% cacao)
- Cooking spray olive oil flavor
- 1 cup water

## Instructions

1. In a large bowl, beat cake mix, water, sour cream, and eggs until well combined.
2. Stir in remaining ingredients until well mixed.
3. Coat a tube pan with cooking spray and pour the cake mixture.
4. Pour the water into your Instant Pot and place a trivet.
5. Place the tube pan over the trivet.
6. Lock lid into place and set on the CAKE setting for 25 minutes.
7. When the timer beeps, naturally release pressure for 5 minutes and quick release remaining pressure.
8. Allow to cool 10 minutes before slicing.
9. Serve.
10. Keep refrigerated.

**Servings:** 12

**Cooking Times**

Total Time: 55 minutes

**Nutrition Facts**

Serving size: 1/12 of a recipe (4.5 ounces)

Percent daily values based on the Reference Daily Intake (RDI) for a 2000 calorie diet.

Nutrition information calculated from recipe ingredients.

**Amount Per Serving**

Calories 399,49

Calories From Fat (47%) 186,48

**% Daily Value**

Total Fat 21,95g 34%

Saturated Fat 6,43g 32%

Cholesterol 57,32mg 19%

Sodium 314,66mg 13%

Potassium 194,68mg 6%

Total Carbohydrates 47,04g 16%

Fiber 3,04g 12%

Sugar 20,77g

Protein 7,62g 15%

# Chocolate Bread with Hazelnuts (Instant Pot)

## Ingredients

- 2 cups flour (all purpose or white whole wheat)
- 1 tsp baking powder
- 1/2 cup sugar
- 1/2 tsp salt
- 1 large egg
- 3/4 cup milk full fat
- 1/2 cup olive oil
- 1 1 cups chocolate chips
- 1 cup hazelnuts, toasted and ground
- 1/2 tsp butter
- 1 cup water

## Ingredients

1. Combine the flour with the baking powder. Add salt and sugar and stir with a spoon.
2. In a separate bowl, beat the egg with a fork, and add milk and the oil.
3. Make a hole in flour, pour the liquid ingredients into solid and stir the mixture.
4. Add chocolate chips and chopped hazelnuts.
5. Grease well and flour a small oblong cake mold and pour the batter.
6. Add water to the inner stainless steel pot in the Instant Pot, and place the trivet inside.
7. Lock lid into place and set on the CAKE and set the mode to "Normal" and the time for 25 minutes.
8. Use Natural Release - it takes 10 - 25 minutes to depressurize naturally.
9. Sprinkle with chopped nuts, slice the bread and serve.

**Servings:** 12

**Cooking Times**

Total Time: 1 hour and 5 minutes

**Nutrition Facts**

Serving size: 1/12 of a recipe (4 ounces)

Percent daily values based on the Reference Daily Intake (RDI) for a 2000 calorie diet.

Nutrition information calculated from recipe ingredients.

**Amount Per Serving**

Calories 386,19

Calories From Fat (51%) 198,57

**% Daily Value**

Total Fat 23,7g 36%

Saturated Fat 5,55g 28%

Cholesterol 16,72mg 6%

Sodium 155,31mg 6%

Potassium 192,44mg 5%

Total Carbohydrates 41,74g 14%

Fiber 3,58g 14%

Sugar 10,08g

Protein 6,9g 14%

# Coffee Chocolate Mint Bundt Cake (Instant Pot)

## Ingredients

- 1 3/4 cups all-purpose flour
- 1 cup granulated sugar
- 3/4 cup cocoa powder ( unsweetened)
- 1 1/2 tsp baking powder
- 1 1/2 tsp baking soda
- 1 tsp salt
- 2 large eggs
- 1 cup buttermilk
- 2/3 cup brown sugar
- 2/3 cup strong brewed coffee
- 1/4 cup butter softened
- 1 Tbsp vanilla extract
- 1 cup semisweet chocolate mini-chips
- 1 Tbsp sifted powdered sugar
- Cooking spray
- 1 cup water

## Instructions

1. Combine the flour, sugar, cocoa powder, baking powder and soda, and salt in a bowl.
2. In a separate bowl, with an electric mixer, whisk eggs, buttermilk, sugar, coffee, butter, vanilla, chocolate chips and powdered sugar.
3. Combine the flour mixture to the egg mixture; beat at HIGH speed for one minute. Coat a non-stick Bundt pan with baking spray and pour the batter.
4. Add water to the inner stainless steel pot in the Instant Pot, and place the trivet inside.

5. Place a bundt pan over the trivet.
6. Lock lid into place and set on the CAKE setting for 25 minutes.
7. Use Natural Release - it takes 10 - 25 minutes to depressurize naturally.
8. Let cool 15 minutes before slicing.
9. Serve.

**Servings:** 16

**Cooking Times**

Total Time: 1 hour and 15 minutes

**Nutrition Facts**

Serving size: 1/16 of a recipe (3.5 ounces)

Percent daily values based on the Reference Daily Intake (RDI) for a 2000 calorie diet.

Nutrition information calculated from recipe ingredients.

**Amount Per Serving**

Calories 237,97

Calories From Fat (27%) 63,14

**% Daily Value**

Total Fat 7,49g 12%

Saturated Fat 4,32g 22%

Cholesterol 31,49mg 10%

Sodium 339,72mg 14%

Potassium 127,3mg 4%

Total Carbohydrates 42,41g 14%

Fiber 2,33g 9%

Sugar 22,83g

Protein 3,99g 8%

# Fast Mayo Chocolate Cake (Instant Pot)

## Ingredients

- 16.5 oz chocolate cake mix
- 1 cup mayonnaise (not include onion or garlic powder)
- 3 eggs
- 1 cup water
- 1 tsp ground cinnamon

## Instructions

1. Whisk cake mix, mayonnaise, water, eggs, and cinnamon in a bowl with electric mixer (low speed).
2. Grease and lightly flour round cake pan.
3. Pour batter into prepared pan.
4. Pour the water into your Instant Pot and place a trivet.
5. Place a cake pan on a trivet.
6. Lock lid into place and set on the CAKE setting for 25 minutes.
7. When the timer beeps, use Natural Release - it takes 10 - 25 minutes to depressurize naturally.
8. Let the pan cool for a few minutes before trying to remove it.
9. Slice, serve and enjoy!
10. Keep refrigerated.

**Servings:** 8

**Cooking Times**

Total Time: 50 minutes

**Nutrition Facts**

Serving size: 1/8 of a recipe (5 ounces).

Percent daily values based on the Reference Daily Intake (RDI) for a 2000 calorie diet.

Nutrition information calculated from recipe ingredients.

**Amount Per Serving**

Calories 401,32

Calories From Fat (39%) 156,39

**% Daily Value**

Total Fat 17,74g 27%

Saturated Fat 4,1g 21%

Cholesterol 77,39mg 26%

Sodium 761,8mg 32%

Potassium 126,51mg 4%

Total Carbohydrates 59,18g 20%

Fiber 2,43g 10%

Sugar 33,97g

Protein 5,22g 10%

# Lucuma and Chia Seeds Pudding (Instant Pot)

## Ingredients

- 1 can (15 oz) coconut milk
- 2 Tbsp Lucuma powder
- 2 sheets of unflavored gelatin (dry mix)

- 1/4 cup chia seeds
- 1/2 cup condensed milk (about 10% fat)

## Instructions

1. Place all ingredients in your Instant Pot's inner pot and give a good stir.
2. Lock lid into place and set on the MANUAL setting for 15 minutes.
3. When the timer beeps, press "Cancel" and carefully flip the Quick Release valve to let the pressure out.
4. Pour the mixture into individual containers and allow to cool before putting them in the refrigerator for at least 2 hours before serving

**Servings:** 4

**Cooking Times**

Total Time: 20 minutes

**Nutrition Facts**

Serving size: 1/4 of a recipe (7.5 ounces)

Percent daily values based on the Reference Daily Intake (RDI) for a 2000 calorie diet.

Nutrition information calculated from recipe ingredients.

**Amount Per Serving**

Calories 590,22

Calories From Fat (45%) 267,58

**% Daily Value**

Total Fat 31,8g 49%

Saturated Fat 22,81g 114%

Cholesterol 13,01mg 4%

Sodium 264,03mg 11%

Potassium 429,03mg 12%

Total Carbohydrates 51,5g 20%

Fiber 7,23g 29%

Sugar 58,28g

Protein 11,52g 23%

# Perfect Tea Cake (Instant Pot)

## Ingredients

- 1/2 cup unsalted butter
- 3/4 cup caster sugar
- 1 egg
- 1 1/2 cups self-raising flour
- 3/4 cup milk
- Topping

- 2 Tbs butter
- 1 Tbs cinnamon
- 1 tsp caster sugar
- Cooking spray butter flavor
- 1 cup water

## Instructions

1. Whisk the butter and sugar with the mixer.
2. Add the egg and continue to beat well. Add a half of the flour to the mixing bowl with half the milk and beat well.
3. Repeat with remaining flour and milk and beat until just smooth.
4. Butter the round cake pan and pour the cake batter.
5. Lock lid into place and set on the CAKE setting for 25 minutes.
6. Use Natural Release - it takes 10 - 25 minutes to depressurize naturally.
7. Transfer the cake to a working surface.
8. While the cake is still hot, spread with butter and sprinkle with cinnamon and sugar.
9. Let cool and serve.

**Servings:** 8

## Cooking Times

Total Time: 55 minutes

## Nutrition Facts

Serving size: 1/8 of a recipe (3.5 ounces)

Percent daily values based on the Reference Daily Intake (RDI) for a 2000 calorie diet.

Nutrition information calculated from recipe ingredients.

## Amount Per Serving

Calories 316,63

Calories From Fat (44%) 138,73

## % Daily Value

Total Fat 15,76g 24%

Saturated Fat 9,64g 48%

Cholesterol 63,22mg 21%

Sodium 28,13mg 1%

Potassium 102,4mg 3%

Total Carbohydrates 40,62g 14%

Fiber 1,15g 5%

Sugar 21,84g

Protein 4,18g 8%

# Sweet Cake Mix  (Instant Pot)

## Ingredients

- 1 box of Beat cake mix (18.5 oz)
- 1/2 cup oil
- 3 whole eggs
- 1 cup water

## Instructions

1. Combine the cake mix, oil and eggs in a mixing bowl.
2. Beat with an electric mixer according to the manufacturer instructions.
3. Pour the batter into the greased cake pan.
4. Cover the cake pan with paper towel and then aluminum foil.
5. Pour the water into your Instant pot and place the cake pan on the trivet.
6. Lock lid into place, press the CAKE mode, set the mode to "Normal".
7. Adjust the cook time to 40 minutes.
8. When the timer beeps, press "Cancel" and use Natural Release - it takes 10 - 25 minutes to depressurize naturally.
9. Remove the aluminum foil and the paper towel and let cool cake for 10 minutes.
10. Slice and serve.

**Servings:** 8

## Cooking Times

Total Time: 1 hour and 25 minutes

**Nutrition Facts**

Serving size: 1/8 of a recipe (4.5 ounces)

Percent daily values based on the Reference Daily Intake (RDI) for a 2000 calorie diet.

Nutrition information calculated from recipe ingredients.

**Amount Per Serving**

Calories 429,11

Calories From Fat (47%) 202,18

**% Daily Value**

Total Fat 22,88g 35%

Saturated Fat 3,59g 18%

Cholesterol 71,06mg 24%

Sodium 458,12mg 19%

Potassium 80,02mg 2%

Total Carbohydrates 51,29g 17%

Fiber 0,72g 3%

Sugar 28,45g

Protein 5,24g 10%

# Total Matte Chocolate Cake (Instant Pot)

## Ingredients

- 4 eggs
- 3/4 cup brown sugar
- 1/4 cup butter softened at room temperature

- 1 cup dark chocolate finely chopped (69% cacao solids)
- 1 cup finely ground almonds
- 1 cup water

## Instructions

1. Whisk eggs with brown sugar in a deep bowl until sugar dissolves completely.
2. Add softened butter and continue to whisk.
3. Add finely chopped chocolate and ground almonds; stir well.
4. Grease a baking pan and pour the chocolate mixture.
5. Add 1 cup water to the inner stainless steel pot in the Instant Pot, and place the trivet inside.
6. Place a baking pan on a trivet.
7. Lock lid into place and set on the CAKE setting for 20 minutes.
8. When the timer beeps use Natural Release.
9. Let cool for 10 minutes and slice.
10. Serve.

**Servings:** 8

**Cooking Times**

Total Time: 40 minutes

**Nutrition Facts**

Serving size: 1/8 of a recipe (4 ounces)

Percent daily values based on the Reference Daily Intake (RDI) for a 2000 calorie diet.

Nutrition information calculated from recipe ingredients.

**Amount Per Serving**

Calories 412,37

**Calories From Fat (57%) 233,36**

**% Daily Value**

Total Fat 26,69g 41%

Saturated Fat 10,63g 53%

Cholesterol 109,75mg 37%

Sodium 45,13mg 2%

Potassium 328,22mg 9%

Total Carbohydrates 37,18g 12%

Fiber 3,88g 16%                    Protein 8,39g 17%

Sugar 30,14g

# Traditional Rice Pudding (Instant Pot)

## Ingredients

- 1 cup basmati rice
- 1 cup condensed milk
- 1 cup almond milk (unsweetened)
- 1 1/4 cups water
- 1/4 cup maple syrup

- 1/8 tsp sea salt
- 3/4 cup heavy cream
- 1 tsp vanilla extract
- 1 tsp cinnamon (or to taste)

## Instructions

1. Place rice in your Instant Pot.
2. Add water, condensed milk, maple syrup, and sea salt.
3. Lock lid into place and set on the PORRIDGE setting for 20 minutes.
4. When the timer beeps, use Natural Release - it takes 10 - 25 minutes to depressurize naturally.
5. Press the Cancel button and open vent.
6. Add cream and vanilla and stir until well mixed.
7. Sprinkle with cinnamon and serve warm or refrigerate for 2 hours.

**Servings:** 6

**Cooking Times**

Total Time: 45 minutes

**Nutrition Facts**

Serving size: 1/6 of a recipe (6.5 ounces)

Percent daily values based on the Reference Daily Intake (RDI) for a 2000 calorie diet.

Nutrition information calculated from recipe ingredients.

**Amount Per Serving**

Calories 339,12

Calories From Fat (40%) 136,88

**% Daily Value**

Total Fat 15,56g 24%

Saturated Fat 9,67g 48%

Cholesterol 58,1mg 19%

Sodium 535,17mg 22%

Potassium 251,96mg 7%

Total Carbohydrates 45,43g 15%

Fiber 0,37g 1%

Sugar 35,82g

Protein 5,41g 11%

# **Conclusion**

As is known to everyone, a vegetarian diet is associated with a higher consumption of fiber, folic acid, vitamins C and E, magnesium, unsaturated fat, and countless phytochemicals.

The health benefits associated with a healthy and well-balanced vegetarian (or vegan) lifestyle are undeniable. Countless studies have shown that a well-planned, nutritious, plant-based diet is associated with a lower risk of obesity, heart disease, diabetes, and stroke, as well as with longer life expectancy.

Vegetarian and vegan diets can be healthy, but they can lack certain nutrients. You may have to use a little creativity to ensure you get enough protein, calcium, iron, and vitamin B12. You can find many of these nutrients in eggs and dairy if you're vegetarian, and from plant sources, if you're vegan.

Made in the USA
Columbia, SC
19 January 2018